OPENING QUOTE

"For as he thinketh in his heart, so is he."

Prefacing

To the woman who has lost key parts of herself by trying to be everything to everyone else, I see you. The woman constantly taking on identities that don't belong to you in an effort to fit in with people who oftentimes just don't appreciate the beauty that you naturally are. I see you working hard to avoid being judged by those who are set in their ways and not open to embracing people with different ideologies and ways of thinking. I see you, afraid to speak up for yourself because of the abuse that you endured for speaking up for yourself in the past. I see you at your "fuck it" moment, no longer wanting to be caught up in a life that was never meant for you, in the process of actively breaking free from anything that keeps you from being able to fully express yourself and live that abundantly healthy and wealthy life you've always known you deserved.

It is my prayer that as you read this book, you will be able to express yourself more freely, do parenting in a way that is meaningful to you, practice your divine spirituality in a way that truly connects you with your life source, find your soul tribe, make better career and relationship choices, live the customized life that you've always desired, and above all have an immensely healthy relationship with yourself before anyone else.

Gratitude

I'm extremely grateful for my children Lizzie, Wes & Marion. Each of you came into my life at critical points, often during a season when I was down on myself and genuinely felt like giving up. It's because of the smiles on your faces and the curiosity that you exuded about life that I became more grounded. It was realizing that you all were watching and learning from me that forced me to take a good and long hard look at myself and gauge whether I would want you to be like me or not.

I'm also immensely grateful to my team of editors, designers, and coaches, Meka Miller, Jessica Raymond, Ronne Brown, Tasha O., Amoya Shante, and more, for believing in me during moments when I found it difficult to believe in myself. Each of you offered correction, coaching, and encouragement that made me look in the mirror and say, "girl stop playing with yourself and the future of you and them babies".

To my mother and siblings, I love every single one of you for always being there through thick and thin. There were moments in my life when I honestly didn't know how I would've moved forward without you. Thank you for seeing me, for supporting me through all of the wild and crazy adventures that I've taken, and for giving me the space to grow and build for the sake of all our futures.

I'm also grateful to all my professors at Huston-Tillotson University and Austin Community College and to the faculty and staff who supported my goals and mentored me when I was in my state of ignorance. Most notably: Dr. Rosalee Martin, for reminding me of my brilliance, Dr. Michael Hirsch, for providing me with opportunities to travel and share my studies in different parts of the States, Dr. Paul Anaejionu, for all the days you allowed me to ask you ridiculous questions in your book crammed office and for lending me the book "As a Man Thinketh" (that book is honestly a huge contributor to me being here today), Dr. Loretta Edelen, for giving me a reason to dream and believe in myself and my abilities, Dr. Connie Pendergrass Williams, for co-creating a space with me for young Black women to thrive and become connected with one another and themselves; I appreciate you for standing strong even when I was weak, Ronnie Washington, for showing me that school didn't have to be such a bore and kept pouring the wisdom into my life, to Dr. Richard Rhodes, for seeing the fire that burned in me and granting me an 'on the spot' scholarship just for sharing my vision, and to all the students who worked alongside me when I started different initiatives that required the buy-in from people outside of myself and everyone who had a significant influence over my success. To Dr. Joyce Olushola Ogunrinde and everyone in our group at the first annual Black Student Athlete Summit, thank you all for pushing me into the spotlight and making it okay to use my voice even though I was one of the most inferior people in the room.

Finally, to all the people who allowed me to invite myself into your important rooms and speak my piece or who made space for me on your coaches, floors, and spare rooms, thank you. Marian Gusseer & family, I love you and thank you so much for loving me as a young girl — same to the Barrientos, Seales, and Villegas families. Marcella Lopez, I love you, girl, and I appreciate you for being such an amazing friend and sister, even through seasons that didn't make sense. Thank you, Yvonne Sanchez, for being the best sponsor I could ever be blessed with and taking this journey with me for YEARS!! To Valerie Mbani for being a wonderful assistant and helping with the first transcription of this book, Annie Vovan

& Shannan Hale for always pulling me into healing spaces, and Kibet Chirchir for becoming an author first and encouraging me through the process. I appreciate y'all tremendously.Finally, to the 2018-2021 CoFo utopian dream team, thanks for being the job that set the standard for what I'm willing to settle for in the world of work; every single one of you forever changed the way I see myself in the workforce and provided the tools needed to help me shape my expectations and desire to only engage in healthy teams and relationships only.

Intro/About Me

At some point in life, we will all undoubtedly arrive at one of our more critical decision-making paths. At the intersection of this path, there is a signpost with three unique directions for us to choose from going forward in life. The first sign which points to the left is the path that majority of people are taking; it is well paved and has little to no surprises along the way. There are pamphlets and guides that give you all the details about how things will go along the path. The second signpost leads to a path straight ahead, and it's a path that you are very familiar with because you've been down that path before. In fact, you've been down that path multiple times, but it always brings you right back to where you are right now, back at the same intersection, trying to decide which way you should go. The third path veers to the right and is the most feared because very few people have ever taken it, and a great deal of those few people couldn't make it through the path without turning around out of fear of the unknown. On this path, there is no guide, no pamphlet, and you only have a few stories from people who have been labeled as "crazy", so you have no idea what to expect. Rumors from the other two paths have been that the third path is dangerous and can lead to some unsafe encounters. So, here you are again faced with deciding whether you'll take the safe path and do what everyone else is doing, take the familiar path that you've been down before,or do something new and venture into the unknown where everything is left up to your discovery with relatively little help along the way. The choice is yours and no one else's, just yours. When you were a child, your parents chose for you; when you first left the care of those who raised you, it was fear that chose. However, now that you are responsible for your path, the question is what will you choose for yourself. Deep down inside, you know you desperately want to take the path that has been less followed - you want to know why the people who take that path come out so different, so seemingly changed in the best of ways. What do you choose?

When I think of a life where we constantly feel stuck, like we can't be ourselves or do the things we truly want to do, I see it as we embark on this journey of choosing our path. As children, that was true, and we didn't have much of a choice depending on those who raised us. However, as we age, we become responsible for ourselves, and the choice increasingly becomes ours to make. Initially, we make those life choices based on the fear we have for the unknown, especially if we were raised by those who feared the unknown, but there comes a point in time where we get tired of walking the same path over and over or doing what everyone else is doing. There comes a point in time where we feel a strong pull towards taking a different path, a path where all the voices of our past and our oppressors become increasingly silent, and the voice of everything we know about ourselves becomes the loudest, protecting us and leading us through our journey every step of the way - even during moments of temporary terror from stepping into the unknown.

It's no coincidence that you're reading this book. I'm of the firm belief that when we choose to take a new path, God/Universe/Creator reveals to us exactly what we need to receive for our next push forward. I can tell you this, the fact that you're reading this book means there is something in your life that you are ready to move past. It could be a situation that you've had enough of but have been too afraid to speak up about or walk away from. It may be a lie that you've been told or have been telling yourself that has consistently kept you from pursuing the things that truly set your soul on fire in the best of ways. Whatever your specific situation is, there's one thing I know for sure, you've had enough of it, and you're ready to step boldly into your next chapter of life, where you get to truly be more of yourself and less of a people-pleaser. You are standing at the proverbial crossroads of life where you have the opportunity to make a new decision, and it is my hope that for once in your life, you will take the path that allows you to discover yourself, your strengths, and your truth like no other.

TABLE OF CONTENTS

HOUSTON, WE HAVE A PROBLEM & AN IDEA

The Point of Enough is Enough

There comes a point in our life when we just get sick and tired of being sick and tired and when we have had absolutely enough of the bullshit. Not only the bullshit that we receive from others but from ourselves as well. We get tired of being in relationships that are out of alignment with our goals, relationships where we're unhappy, feel unloved, unworthy, and unseen. We get tired of getting into jobs and business situations where we feel like we are not being paid enough, or our time is not valued, or we're not respected, or we're not heard or able to put our voice into important areas, and we genuinely become tired of living a life that does not line up with the life we're holding in our hearts. It's like we have one lifestyle inside our hearts, yet on the outside, we're living something completely different. When you realize this doesn't line up, or this is not matching, then that's when you realize you've had enough, and that's the most amazing time to start making moves and actions towards upgrading yourself and changing your life.

Where I find many of us go wrong once we've had enough of a situation or a person is when we try to force the situation or person to change itself instead of looking at our own habits and behaviors that are constantly leading us into things that don't align with what we really want. For example, when you get into a relationship or you're dating someone, and that person is toxic and makes you feel like shit because you enjoy the idea of being in a relationship, you endure the hurt and pain, but what you do when you're fed up is to walk away feeling like the person was the problem when in reality that person was really just being who they were. That's who they are at this stage of their life. We walk away feeling like they're the ones who need to change. We walk away with narratives in our heads like "all men are trash" when in reality, the common denominator between us and trash men is "us". For example, when we find ourselves walking away from one relationship to another and the outcome is similar to the one we left, we think, "oh my God, these people are so toxic", but we really should be looking in the mirror because this is what we are personally attracted to. As we dive into this book, I want you to understand that this journey toward becoming more of yourself and less of a people-pleaser is about you. It's not about finding a way to get the people around you to become better. Instead, it's about finding a way to become better for yourself so that you find people who are better aligned with you and who don't need to be changed to fit your personal worldview. This is truly a journey where I hope you get aligned with yourself so that you don't enter similar situations repeatedly where you continue to attract what you don't want in life but rather attract more of what you desire. You won't be able to change until you own up to who you are, what you want out of life, the behaviors that you are perpetrating, your patterns, and all these things that keep coming up time and again. My goal is to share personal stories and tips/tools that will help you shift into who it is that you are ready and desire to be so that you can get out of repeated cycles of toxicity and dissatisfaction and then move towards what means the most for you.

Now that I've got you here, I want to tell you about my own personal "enough is enough" moment, the final moment when I realized I was the problem. Before I dive into my story, please know that we will have many moments in our lives where we become fed up with outdated situations, and the difference between staying stuck in them and being freed from the cycles is how we choose to respond to the situation. Do we use the usual tactics that have not gotten anywhere, or do we switch things up and try something different?

From mid to late 2021 through early 2022, I got myself into a few situations. I was eager to win in those years, and I was so ambitious. I decided I was going to go full-time as a coach, working in my own practice and setting my mind on that. So, I went out and started building my brand and working with a business coach to really help me push my goals forward and build a structure to the point where I could operate as a business that actually worked and also had good processes. I also decided in the same year that I was going to do something different in my dating life because it was basically bullshit, and the little that I had going on wasn't what I wanted, so I decided that I would actually date-date somebody. I ended up meeting a guy who wasn't really my type, but my then therapist encouraged me to try something different with someone who wasn't my type, so I moved forward with dating him anyway — even though I wasn't feeling it totally. I had wanted to work through the things that were continuously getting me into certain cycles, so I went forward with dating him. A part of me wanted to take on the business and the relationship as a way to serve as an example for young girls, teen moms, and single mothers who thought their lives couldn't amount to anything simply because of decisions they made in their pasts. I wanted to use my life as a living example to show them that you can move from being in poverty and work your way up to having abundance. I wanted to show them that they could go from being just an employee to a business owner and a single mom to a good solid relationship. So, I wanted to demonstrate that a woman could achieve all these things. However, I had a problem in my real life that I had to come to terms with. Although I had the business, relationship, and high-class coach, I wasn't happy with whom I was. I didn't like how my business life was going or the way my coach wanted me to move, my parenting was crappy because my kids were on the back burner, and I didn't even like the guy I was dating; it was like having an extra child who needed far more attention than the existing three kids I have combined. My life was a mess; I found myself constantly burning out, losing interest in the things I loved, unable to express my creativity, drained, agitated, irritated, and dying on the inside with a smile on my face externally. I had started questioning everything I was doing and asking myself, does this line up with the life I truly want, or do I just make it seem like it on the outside? It was like while I was trying to portray this image where I could say, "look, mama, I made it," and "hey, single moms, we can do this", it was like my actual life internally was filled with struggles and suffering, and I hated it. I felt fake — like I was pushing this image of myself that was great, but it just didn't reflect my reality. From working with my coach, it was like this wasn't the type of person I needed to learn from or do business with; from industry misalignment to how we actually operated and ran our businesses and the cultural misalignment, it wasn't me, and I couldn't do it. In the relationship, I realized I was so tired of trying to cater to every need of someone who needed to know where I was constantly, what I was doing, who I was with, and if he wasn't there with me, he needed to be on the phone seven days a week. I got tired of this shit; this wasn't the life I wanted. I didn't want to be around people who constantly sucked energy from me and attempted to control my life and what success should look like for me. I didn't want any of that, and it was not working for me as a woman, a mother, and a lady who wanted to lead an honest and authentic business life. When January 2022 came, I decided that I was done trying to force myself to work together and be in relationships with people who were not right for me in order to hold up an image that painted me as fully being someone that I had not fully stepped into at the time.

When we try to portray an image where we are something that we're not, it's hard for us to build genuine connections with people who are right for our journey. Imagine how hard it is to tell everyone, "oh hey, my business is suffering, and I need help," when you've been walking around like your shit was all the way together, but it wasn't. It just doesn't work like that, and it can be incredibly embarrassing. It was time for me to seriously evaluate my life and change the way that I had been doing just about everything. After breaking everything off with almost everything, I didn't know what the way forward would look like, but I knew I needed to move away from people who were incompatible with my desired way of life. So, I cut everything off and thought I'd go back to life as usual, before the coach and before the dating situationship. I figured I'd find out how to do business on my own, make up for the lost time with my kids, and become a better mother and have a better life. I had no true plan, and I would've most definitely fallen back into my former patterns, but God had something different in store for me that completely changed the way that I saw the impact of the decisions I was making and the role I was playing in, which constantly caused my life to be in shambles.

After about a week that I broke things off with this guy, he went crazy. He was reaching out to my ex-husband and his wife, and he was reaching out to my friends, making fake profiles, inquiring about me and a guy that I had absolutely nothing to do with and didn't even know outside of an encounter with a group of my friends. This guy had gone mad, making up stories about me and telling lies and a bunch of bullcrap. Once he realized that my friends and family weren't going to entertain him and his smear campaign, he started stalking me. He started showing up in places that I frequented but were out of his way. He would show up at my door in the middle of the night saying he wanted to talk, and he showed up at the trail that I walked on, the store I went to, and was spotted on multiple occasions hanging out at my apartments. There was even a time when he literally popped out from the side of my apartment building when I was leaving. It freaked me out so much that my co-parents even felt like the kids and I were unsafe and offered to make space for all of us at their home about four hours away until all this passed over, and this guy got his emotions in check. It was such an embarrassing and confusing time for me, but it spoke directly to my decision-making habits.

In that season, I had been in and out of toxic or misaligned relationships of all sorts just to uphold an image and feel like I was doing something. I was over it; I was literally done putting myself in unstable situations just because I didn't want to take the time to do the internal work that was necessary for me to move away from what I didn't want and toward what I did want. After all was said and done, I moved away from the United States and went to Mexico just so I could clear my head and think through what I needed to do going forward without all the extra noise of life back home. I spent time in solitude, reflecting and focusing on myself. This was where I discovered I was the problem, and I had not been paying attention to what I was involving myself in because I was so focused on the shallow parts of things instead of being patient and ensuring we were compatible with achieving similar goals. I focused so much on the outside that I was completely neglecting doing the internal work so that I could actually do better and not just look like I was doing better.

So many of you out there are having similar situations but just in different areas of your life. For some of you, it may be simple as not being able to show up fully around family members who don't get you. For others, it may be that you keep accepting less than you deserve from friends and even yourself. At any rate, you feel like you're not able to express yourself and have the types of relationships that you really want. One thing that I was lacking as I was getting into these different situations was a solid vision for myself. I didn't know what I wanted, and when we don't know what we want, or we only know what we don't want, many things will come our way, and we won't know how to discern between what's best for us and our future. This often leads us to accept behaviors and positions that drain us more than they energize us. Like I mentioned in the beginning, we can get to these "Enough is enough" stages many times in our life, but until we know what we actually want in place of the other things that we don't want, then we will likely continue to get more of the same thing we've been getting but just with a different face or name.

What Do You Really Want in Life? (Write the Vision)

Until we can identify what we actually want in this life and make it clear to ourselves and others, we will constantly find ourselves in less-than-desirable situations where our needs are not being met. So, it's important for us to establish an idea of what we want if we really want to change the course and trajectory of our lives and the relationships we have with our family members, friends, and the jobs that we have and the work that we do in this world.

The big question in this chapter is, "What do you really want in this life?" In the previous chapter, I talked about how it's hard for us to move forward if we don't know what we're moving towards. It's hard for us to get out of the cycles and patterns of dissatisfaction and choosing things that aren't giving us what we need if we don't know what we actually want and need. So, if you find yourself ending up in these less-than-desirable situations, then you've gotta look at yourself and ask yourself what you actually want. This is extremely important. We have to know what kind of life it is that we want to live and how we want things to be around us. If you have no interest in going around in circles and continuously changing out the people and the jobs only to land in the same situation, then we're going to connect with ourselves on a different level so that we can make it clear for ourselves to know who's for us and who's not for us, and what's for us and what's not for us. The only way to get to that point is by coming up with an idea of your ideal life. You've gotta sit down and map out who the fuck you are, who you want to be, and how you want to live life.

Then you've gotta do it for you, not for people on the outside, not so you can get claps and cookies and celebration and acceptance from people on the outside, but because you have a vision that's important for you. As you go through this section, think about who you are. When you get to be your most authentic self, and you are around the people who truly support you and care about you, who are you? What are the things that are important to you, what are the things that make you happy, and if you didn't have to prove anything to anyone, how would you react in certain situations — namely, the situations that you're in right now that you're dissatisfied with? For me, cutting off the relationships I talked about in the former chapter happened because I realized I wanted healthier relationships where I could be my true self and still be respected, trusted, loved, and heard. I wanted to have a relationship where my voice and needs mattered just as much as the other person's voice and needs mattered. So, I had to get dreamy with things and tap into my bank of imagination where I imagined what my life would be like if I didn't have to worry about other people judging me, and then I had to let that vision be my guide.

Use Your Imagination

A lot of us don't realize the value of using our imagination. In fact, we've been taught to believe that it's child's play, something that's only done by children and useless to adults. However, that's not the case because imagination is used in everything that we do and is the number one tool used for creativity and innovation. It is literally the life blood for being able to make changes in our lives by allowing us to come up with new ideas and thinking up new solutions to our problems. Utilizing my imagination has literally contributed to my growth significantly. Imagination was how I was able to rethink my life and dream up a new way of living.

Let's take it to another level. If you ever find yourself daydreaming, what you're often doing is escaping from a reality that doesn't align with what you want and entering an alternate reality where you are better able to express yourself and think up how things could be different. The problem arises when we leave our imagination and write it off as if it doesn't connect to our reality. It does. I must say that all the things we imagine are not necessarily what we desire, but some of our imaginations and daydreaming come from a place of wounds and pain, so knowing the difference before mapping out your vision using the imagination method is important.

This may sound silly to some of you because we tend to think our vision and dreams are things that happen outside of ourselves, and we tend to look outwardly in an attempt to find what we want in life, but this is a process that is 100% governed by you. This is why I'm making it a point to mention imagination in this book as a tool that will help you rethink your life, your limitations, and how far you can really go. We are all creators, and the creation process begins with our ideas, which are the things we hold within. So, as you embark on this journey of really stepping into yourself and owning who you are, it's important that you tap into the source which is within you and not governed by anyone outside your own self. Try your imagination out. Next time you are facing an issue, pay attention to your thoughts and where your mind goes. How are you handling problems in your head, and are you able to see a resolution? It's also important to know that as you use your imagination, you must focus on changing your own behavior and reactions because if you focus on changing others, then you will likely fail because you have little to no control over another person and their reactions. We only have power over our own behavior.

When thoughts constantly come up while you're in the midst of an unpleasant situation, pay attention to them and what they tell you. Don't act on them immediately, but observe them and see if they are trying to lead you to a solution. When I recall past jobs where I was dissatisfied, I remember being at work, but my mind would be on other things like working with a team that I could laugh and enjoy life with while working towards a greater goal. I would think about having the freedom to dress how I wanted, have flexibility in my work schedule, and what it would be like to have ample paid time off. Once I paid attention to this recurring thought, I started Googling workplaces near me that embodied those characteristics I kept imagining, and within a few months, I found myself in a role with an extremely amazing team at a job that I like to refer to as the "Utopian" workplace. It went against so many workplace norms and put people first. We had parties multiple times per year, played games with one another, normalized regular non-work related social hours, and everyone had a voice at the table of the business. It was surreal and something that I had literally dreamed up, searched, and found. The same thing goes for landing my highest-paying job. I imagined myself having more financial freedom and abundance, and then I searched until I found it. I hope you see the power of imagination. Many people have used it to create a life that truly aligns with their wildest dreams. Look at the clothes on your body, the cars you drive, the houses and buildings that surround us, and the cell phone and tech gadgets that you use regularly. All of these things came from someone's imagination.

The Vision is for You

As you are writing out your vision, I want to remind you that the vision is for you. Be careful who you share it with before you are ready to act on it. Everyone will not believe it's possible, and many people will think it's crazy or you're crazy for thinking you could have a life that's different from what THEY imagined for you or believe is possible for themselves. In the same way that you must guard your focus, you must guard your vision and keep it between you and those who are headed in the same direction as you or who get it. Mapping out your life vision - even if it's in simple areas - is a time for you to exercise your creativity in a safe space. Without removing the permanent parts of your life like children, race, etc., play around with how you want your life to look, and then write it out in a private journal or a digital doc that's only accessible to you. Then begin taking inspired actions towards your vision. This means doing things that align with the truth of who you really are. These are actions that are not done from a place of fear or desire to please/gain the approval of people outside. This is you showing up to conversations and situations and relationships fully as yourself without the need to mask who you truly are in an effort to appear more appealing to another.

Having a vision is important because it serves as a roadmap to the types of behaviors and actions we need to take in order to live the life we desire. Earlier in this book, I talked about entering relationships and business agreements only to appear a certain way to the outside world. Now that I have more clarity about who I want to be in life, I know that I can no longer accept any business offer or relationship just because it will make me "look" good on the outside, or elevate my broken sense of importance. . I've learned that saying no is an extremely powerful action toward getting what we truly want, even when the offer is compelling. For example, in 2022, one of my very successful friends created a new program that had many amazing perks and would have given me access to celebrity-level clientele. The only problem was that, although the program was amazing and had a ton of value, it was not aligned with my vision at the time. Celebrity clientele and some of the other perks of the program were attractive. However, they would've moved me away from my true goals and not toward them. In that season, I needed to take action toward the goals that I had already set out for myself and not go through another program to create more goals and learn. I had a similar situation with a relationship where someone from my past came around and was ready to pursue something further with me. It was a great offer, and it hit on my desire to be in a long-term committed relationship that led to marriage. However, he was no longer in alignment with what I needed in a partner. By having a vision, I became more aware of the fact that my idea of a healthy relationship was less about the idea of the relationship and more about how the partnership with another person could mutually move us towards a life we can both be proud of holistically, without seeking to convince the other person that they should change to become anyone other than who they are.

As you become the best version of yourself, many offers will come your way, which will be tempting. It is up to you to take the time to figure out if they are what you really need to get to where you want to go. It will be up to you to not act impulsively but rather pay more attention to what you agree to and whether that lines up with what you want out of life.

Get into this mindset where you realize stepping into your real self is going to require you to move in a way that you've dreamed of, and it won't always make sense to those outside. This doesn't mean you can't be yourself, but it simply means you will have to reacquaint some people with who you are and what you're doing now going forward, regardless if they believe in you or think it's a worthless journey. Don't allow anyone to talk you out of what you see as possible for yourself. Instead, do the hard work that will move you toward where you truly want to be in life.

SECTION 2:

WHAT'S STOPPING YOU

As we embark on this journey towards becoming our real selves, there will be lots of roadblocks ahead that may discourage us from being our true selves if we don't understand them and why they arise. In this section, we'll focus on recognizing some of the roadblocks that may present themselves and what we can do to move forward in spite of them.

Fear of Judgment and Rejection

One of the biggest blocks that come between us being ourselves, speaking up for our needs, and doing the things we love is the fear of being judged and rejected. Think about it; it's why people who identify as LGBTQ+ have a hard time coming out to their families because they know a lot of judgment and attempts to "fix" them will follow. It was the same thing that happened to me when I decided to participate in a religion that was different from what my family and friends were used to. It took time for me to tell everyone because I was afraid of what they would say. After all, I was signing up for a religion that had a very negative image in the west as being intolerant, unfriendly to women, and murderous over their religion. Telling my family and friends was hard. I questioned myself regularly and tried to find the right words to let them know that I was still me because I didn't want them to mistake me as an extremist or any other crazy thing that I had heard about Muslims growing up. Telling my family was the easiest part because these are people who have known me my whole life and have a good grip on my character outside of labels. It was telling my group of friends, who were mostly Christian women, where things got really shaky. Some of them were upset, others were holding prayer groups for my healing, and some had the balls to address me directly to tell me how they thought I was sick and under attack by the devil. Others didn't skip a beat on the opportunity to question my motives and argue with me about how I was going to hell and was now unlovable by God because I was an unbeliever. They constantly did what they could to remind me that I needed to return to my former ways because I was lost. It was honestly one of the most difficult times of my life, and I constantly found myself wanting to go back to the religion, not because I felt like it was what was right for me, but because I was tired of being rejected by those who I had built a community with. I no longer wanted to be seen as the unbeliever who was going to hell and should be avoided like the plague so I wouldn't infect those around me with whatever spiritual illness they thought I had because I chose to follow a different path toward understanding my relationship with God and others. At the time, I couldn't see how much of a blessing this season was for me. I literally found out who my true friends were; they understood me and supported me during a season of change that even I didn't understand. It was like

God's way of waking me up from my complacency and showing me which people really stood by me for who I was and those who only stood by me when I matched their agenda. I was upset for a while, but then I grew up to understand that those people had every right to exclude me from their life because I was in violation of their own personal beliefs about righteousness, and it wasn't my job to convince them that they should accept me or change myself in order to be accepted by them.

I know so many of us fear judgment and rejection, but I think these are great opportunities for us to identify our real friends going forward. There were people who knew me as both a Christian and a Muslim who never treated me any differently based on either title. As I did what felt best for me openly, and standing firm in my decision allowed me to clearly see who my friends were. These were people who weren't going to judge me or avoid me because I chose to embody a belief system that was foreign to them. I would say that when we're coming out as our authentic selves, it's important to know that some people will temporarily be confused but will eventually come back around. Some will stick around and support us through the change, while others won't want to be around us until we go back to our former ways. Be warned that you shouldn't return to who you were before simply to keep those around who disagree with who you're being. Instead, nurture the relationship you have with those who are there for you without any expectations. Being judged and rejected is hard, but it's honestly harder pretending to be someone we're not and always biting our tongue to keep people around who simply don't want to be or don't need to be around us. Judgment and rejection serve as our protection from being surrounded by misaligned people and those who refuse to take the time to embrace difference. Had I allowed my former friends to talk me out of my decision by way of judgment and rejection, there are some beautiful experiences and epiphanies that I wouldn't have had that have literally opened my eyes to life in a completely new manner and allowed me to truly appreciate creation.

Environment & Exposure

Our families, homes, friends, and local neighborhoods all play an essential role in developing our belief systems about who we can be, who's worthy of what, and what's acceptable to do in life. If you grew up in a closed environment where there is little diversity, and the majority of the people like you live in a certain way, there's a high chance that you'll have trouble believing you can do anything different in life.

As an example, I was born in a small rural Texas town where it wasn't common for Black and Latino people to be educated or pursue certain professions. Most people believed college was too expensive and that having a business of their own or working in certain fields was out of their reach. People rarely moved outside of that narrative and often talked negatively about those who did and succeeded, especially women. It was a long-held belief that school and certain jobs weren't for people of color. They also tended to be closed-minded to people of different nationalities and religious beliefs that were not commonly found in the small town and surrounding areas. People who grew up in these environments where they were less exposed to the outside world tended to hold beliefs that doing things outside of what they were used to was something that was reserved for white or rich people and thus rarely pursued life outside of what they were used to.

Growing up, I had the privilege of living in Minneapolis, Minnesota, which was the complete opposite of my small country hometown. There were so many people from so many different parts of the world who spoke different languages and had different beliefs. Initially, it was uncomfortable to embrace all of them because I heard those people were all non-believers who'd go to hell, but once I started befriending students who were different from me and visiting their homes, I realized they were also humans, just like me. Some were good people, and others weren't, but there was nothing inherently wrong with them just because they held different beliefs or came from different backgrounds.

It was in the big city that I was exposed to successful Black people and kids who believed they could be anything. It was the first place where I saw families from all backgrounds living in the same neighborhoods and mingling with each other outside of the town's sporting events. My mind was opened to the idea that small-town life wasn't all there was. However, there were some beliefs that still embedded themselves around me because of my family's personal beliefs. For example, the idea that those who committed pre-marital sex deserved punishment and were hated by God, and the idea that women who became teen or single moms were damaged goods who wouldn't amount to anything, were some of the beliefs. These are the beliefs that personally held me back from initially pursuing the life that I wanted because I hadn't been exposed to anything different. The teen and single moms that I knew were all living in poverty and had pretty toxic lifestyles. So, naturally, when I grew up and became a teen then a single mom myself, I boxed myself into this group of people who were incapable of doing anything for themselves because the dominant narrative and theme from my environment were negative. I actually behaved in a way that mirrored the stereotypical image of a single mom because I did not know there was any other way, and the people around me only affirmed that I had ruined my life and would no longer be able to live a good life. Obviously, I didn't fall for that for too long because I went on to do things differently in spite of what was said about "people like me". The point of this section is to make you aware of the fact that sometimes our environments have such an influence and opinion about how life is supposed to be lived and what's right or wrong that we are tempted to believe that it knows best about us and the world around us when it oftentimes it doesn't. Our environment is based on a limited or controlled understanding of the world around us.

Regardless of our environment and what's typical or acceptable and unacceptable, at some point in our lives, we have to realize that just because things don't work in one environment does not mean that they won't work in another, nor does it also mean that we won't have anyone to support us if we choose to live life differently. Don't allow the environment you grew up in or your lack of exposure to make you feel like your dream self and lifestyle are too big or out of reach. Always ask yourself the question, "who is my dream or vision too big or too much for, and is this real or just the way that this particular group of people or person thinks?" Many of us will be tempted to sell ourselves short and continue accepting less than we want and deserve because we have yet to see it done differently around us. It is your duty to be the difference that you want to see in the world. It takes one person to make a change and introduce a new way of life or different belief for others to begin experiencing liberation from old narratives and ways of doing things. Sometimes we simply need to change our environment in order to change our lives and get around people who are already living in a reality that is similar to the one we want.

Patterns

Our patterns are the behaviors that we repeat over and over again with new people in our lives, often expecting a different outcome. At the beginning of this book, I talked about how we sometimes leave one toxic relationship or situation and enter another relationship, expecting things to be different simply because it's new, yet we find ourselves in a similar position as before, leaving us confused. The saying "all men are dogs" can be credited to someone who is operating within a toxic pattern where they likely aren't taking responsibility for their dating habits and behaviors. When we are unaware of patterns and the role of patterns, the chances of us repeating them are high. Patterns are often picked up during childhood or adolescence when we're still learning about the world around us, and they can be as simple as saying we like one color when we like another to fit in or as complex as blaming other people for the things that go wrong in life. To pinpoint your patterns, look at the parts of your life that you find yourself continuously struggling in. Do you constantly find yourself ending up in friendships with people who aren't trustworthy or gossipers? Are you getting into jobs where you're not paid your worth? Or entering relationships where you end up feeling used? It's likely directly related to a pattern that you're subconsciously engaging in, like ignoring red flags in potential friendships and relationships or failing to really pay attention to whether a job or conversation is right for you. Sometimes we have negative patterns where we surround ourselves with people who are out of our alignment in order to prove that we are worthy. At any rate, you should really look at your life and figure out where you are failing to be truthful with yourself about the usefulness of a certain pattern or behavior that you use in situations that are difficult or where you want to prove yourself worthy. Remember, you are already worthy, but you have to put yourself in situations where you do not have to force people to like you or convince them that you are good enough for them.

One of my biggest patterns was the pattern of dating unavailable men. They would practically tell me that they weren't interested in anything more than friendship or a friends-with-benefits setup, and I would agree, but then I try to do things in the relationship with them to convince them that they needed to make up their minds and either be with me or not. The pattern I had was expecting to be able to change someone's mind when they already had it made up instead of seeing my worth and walking away. In my work life, I had this pattern of applying to jobs that I knew I didn't want outside of the amount of money they were able to offer. So when I landed the job and later realized that I wasn't being paid my worth, I would get mad, failing to acknowledge the fact that it was me who applied to this role, to begin with, and failing to be real about my financial needs and needs in a workplace. This resulted in so much dissatisfaction and lots of roles that I was misaligned with. I had a high turnover in my relationships and work life because I was continually employing the same behaviors but expecting different results.

Life doesn't work like that. In order to break the patterns, we have to become more active participants in our relationships and life. We should be realistic about our needs and know when to speak up or walk away from something that is clearly out of our alignment. We have to take more responsibility for ourselves and not expect other people to give us anything that we aren't willing to give ourselves. If we want more truth, we need to be more truthful to ourselves. If we want better jobs, we need to be real about our interests. For better relationships with family members and friends, we need to have more difficult conversations and stop expecting people to read our minds and know what we want. We have to change in order for our situations to change by breaking useless patterns and moving away from behaviors that push us away from our goals.

Fear of Failure

So many of us refuse to put ourselves out there and try something new out of fear of failure. We think to ourselves, what if I try it and I don't get it right on the first try? We think about how people may judge us because we did something different and ended up looking like a loser. I struggled with this early on in my business, which is why it was so hard for me to tell the truth about the state of my business because I didn't want to appear to be a failure or someone who got it wrong and didn't know what I was doing. I didn't want to appear as someone who tried doing something different and just proved to the rest of the world why people like me shouldn't do certain things because we don't know what we're doing. This is such a flawed way of thinking because it assumes that we must know exactly what we're doing to be worthy of pursuing an idea or way of life that we want to pursue. It assumes that we are supposed to know how to do things before we even get started, which goes directly against how we as humans learn and actually figure out how to do new things. Could you imagine a baby who knew they couldn't walk but felt like they should know how to walk and chose to not try walking simply because they didn't know how and would look like a fool if they did? Foolish right? That's how it looks when we expect ourselves to know how to do things that we were never taught to do. We look foolish when we expect to be great at something that we are just now learning how to do. In 2022, I was ashamed to talk about the state of my business because it wasn't operating the way that I thought it should be. However, it was still new, and I was a first-generation business owner operating with minimal understanding of how businesses worked; of course, I was prone to failing. I didn't know what I was doing. I did just that, and my business failed miserably; however, I learned a lot of lessons along the way about how I could do business better going forward. It was through the failures that I was able to see what I was missing. It was because I had trouble sourcing and retaining clients that I was able to see that I needed processes for that. The trial and error that I was so afraid to go through because of thoughts like, "what a shame that I didn't know how to do business in the first year", was exactly what I needed to figure out how to do business better and start succeeding.

We fear failure because we think it will make us look bad or ignorant, like we don't know what we're doing, but we should actually enjoy it because it is the most useful feedback mechanism that often comes without the price tag that a formal education over the same topics might come at. When we move away from fearing failure, it is easier to step into ourselves and learn more about life and the world around us. It has been through my failures that I have learned the most lessons about life. When my first marriage failed, I learned more about what I did and did not want in a relationship. When I failed to be a "good" Muslim and Christian, I learned so much about the religious community from multiple angles that opened my mind up to the concept of God in a way that I would've never expected had I not taken those leaps. The same thing happened at the last job I held when I failed to meet the company's standards. I learned a lesson about why it was so important to prioritize and not blindly apply to roles just because they offered a nice title and lovely pay. I learned that it was so much more important to know how well things fit me instead of trying to fit myself into places that didn't necessarily align.

I hope you realize failure plays an important role in our development process. It is through failure that we learn the most about what works and what doesn't work for us. Our failures allow us to adjust our lives for the better. Think about babies again; they fail miserably in the walking and crawling phase, but every time they get up and try again, they try a new strategy or method that usually works better than the last time, and they do that until they figure out what works and are able to confidently walk. When you are in the early stages of shifting your life to be in alignment with what you want, you are like a baby all over again, falling down and having to get back up and try again until you figure out what works for you and can do it with confidence. Be patient and keep trying. Eventually, you will get it — whatever it is for you. The people who are really successful in life will not make you feel bad about failing. Have you ever seen an adult shame a baby for not figuring out how to walk on the first day or within the first few months that they try to walk? No! So understand that the only people who laugh at you or talk down on you when you're in your beginning phases are often those who have not done what you're doing for themselves.

To wrap this section up, be aware that your own behaviors, your traumas, your tendency to please people, your desire to see other people happy over your own happiness, the fear of failure and judgment, the remnants of messages from your environment and lack of exposure to a different way of life, all play a role in distracting yourself from getting what you want in life if you're not aware of them. These are all very real parts of why it's hard for you to express yourself in the way that you really want to express yourself. It's important that you go into new situations understanding that there are things from your upbringing and past that will make it challenging for you, and regardless of those things, it's your responsibility to move forward and choose yourself every single time. There will be thoughts, narratives, and fears that simply won't serve you and that's ok. Choose what works for you and do it with consideration for your future self. You don't have to do things how they've always been done or how they're expected to be done by people outside.

SECTION 3:

WORTH IT

In the previous chapter, I talked about ultimately recognizing that what you want to do is valid and will almost always go against the grain of what you're used to, but it's still valid, regardless of if you simply want to have better relationships with your children, spouse or self, or regardless of what your goal is if you have an idea, vision or dream. That thing is in you for a reason. It's there because it is dear to you, and it's something that you value and want in your life. So, I want you to understand that your vision is worth pursuing. Even though there will be roadblocks and things may get hard at times, and you'll probably engage in self-sabotaging behavior, you've gotta recognize that because you hold the vision of living life in a new way for yourself and generations to come, and because it is something that makes you happy when you dream about it, it's worth you investing your time, money, effort, and energy into it regardless of what other people will say. Worrying about what other people will say is what gets us caught up all the time. Worrying about how we'll be judged or how other people are going to feel if we do something that's different gets us caught up all the time.

So, as you embark on making whatever dream or vision it is that you have in your heart right now a reality, it is essential for you to cut out the loser behavior that you're participating in where you constantly end up with the losing hand in every situation because you refuse to stand up for who you really are and what you want. You have to treat your dreams as if they are worth defending with your actions and behaviors. You've gotta grab that vision and say, "this is worth much more to me than the temporary pain or grief that I'll feel when a potential friend, family member, or date won't be happy with my decision". You have to remind yourself that your vision is worth more to you than your fears. You have to bring faith into your vision because how can it come into reality if you don't believe that it can come into reality? You have to believe that what you are pursuing is worth it, that you are worth it, and that because God gave you the vision to pursue, then it is something that is worth your pursuit.

The things you want in your life are what you genuinely want around you. When you start moving towards them, your life will start sprouting and opening up like a beautiful flower because you will start behaving in a manner that aligns with your truth. You'll be less stressed out about life because you'll know that you are genuinely moving towards things that align with what you want in life. You'll know how to set better boundaries and lay down the foundation, so you don't have to worry too much about things you don't want, and you'll rather spend less time around misaligned people. When you hold on to your vision and you start becoming yourself, you're better able to discern what goes against it.

Back to healthy relationships, as my vision for healthy relationships becomes clearer, I have a better understanding of why I can't entertain certain types of behaviors and involve myself deeply with people who don't prioritize healthy relationships. So, I want you to really sit with yourself and sit with your vision once you've written out what you want in this life and what's important for you in this life. Sit with it and affirm it, speak your vision into your life as if it's already real, and walk around as if who you are (want to be) isn't some far-off dream but is already here with you based on a shift in your behaviors and a shift in the stories that you're telling yourself, and also based on a shift in what you accept and allow into your life from other people.

We've really gotta rewrite the narrative; this is our story, and our life is our living story. We are the living story, the living testimony, and if we want our life to turn out a certain way, then we've gotta take back the pen and be the author and narrator of our story deciding how things will go. Will you continue to be the person who always accepted less than you deserved, always in toxic situations, never really living life the way you want to, doing the things you don't want to, or will you wake up and say, "fuck all this I'm going to live how I want to live and make amazing memories with beautiful people who see me". You have to decide whether you'll hang around people who have a similar vision as yourself and are as faithful to their vision as you are. You have to get to the point where you stop trying to prove yourself to people who refuse to see you and rather show up only for those who get you and are around you. We've gotta start telling the story how we want to tell it and recognize that our story is written directly through our actions. It doesn't have to be some Disney dream, woo woo shit. Getting the life we want is ultimately up to us, and we have more control than we think.

One thing that really helped me understand the importance of taking my life back and living it the way that I said I wanted to live it was when I realized that my children are watching everything that I do and are directly learning from me what they're capable of. My actions and behaviors directly influence what they'll believe they can do in their own lives. I had to zoom out and look at the big picture, which included analyzing the fact that if I continued to accept toxic things in my life or say I wanted to do things but never did them, my kids would likely grow up the same way and never get around to living their ideal lives or doing the things they wanted to do. I had to start putting action with my words. When I say I want to do something, I put it into action, but I also make sure that it's healthy, good, and true to me or real to the life that I want. I do this because I realize there are people who are watching me. There are people who I am their role model in their life regardless of if I want to admit it or like it or not. I am somebody's role model, and what I decide to do with my life will serve as a direct example of what they believe they can do in their lives. If they see me and know that I've been through crazy stuff, but I still persevered and did what I needed to do to overcome and live a happy, healthy life that aligned with my truth, they'll know it's possible for them too. It's representation. You become the representative for those who want to do what you're saying you want to do but have not done it yet. Be a good representative of your word, your needs, your desires, and yourself. It shows that you can do something amazing and different. Show that you can do things first, and I can guarantee you that the other people around you will start getting it. What we often do wrong, at least in my case, is trying to get other people to do something different before I also do something different. I would try to convince people to follow along with the idea that I had before because I wanted to see somebody else do it first before me just to see if it was safe, but sometimes you've gotta be the first to do it. You have to prove to yourself that you can do it, and then other people who you want to be on your journey may naturally follow.

Rewrite the narrative, take control of your story, and take your power back. Don't allow other people to dictate what happens in your life by telling you what you can and cannot do and what you do and don't deserve. Be very careful about whose voice you listen to because people are humans just like you and not God. What gives them more say over your future than you?

SECTION 4:

THE WAY FORWARD

Our Social Circle Matters

A huge essential part of your journey forward and toward making the life that you want to see in reality are to control the people that you have surrounding you. They matter significantly. If you have people around you who are always negative and planting seeds of doubt in you, questioning what you're doing, or making you feel like you're not worthy of doing something, it will most definitely poison your dreams and vision, making you feel like what you are pursuing is something that is out of your reach. If you spend enough time around them, you will start to believe them, and you'll find yourself stuck because you're allowing someone else to dictate to you. Your social circle matters because the conversations you have with the people around you impact your level of energy and the beliefs you have about the things that you want to do. It can be either discouraging or encouraging, and when you're making big shifts and changes in your life, you have to make sure that you are around people who will lift you up and remind you of how amazing and worthy you are to pursue a life that is meaningful to you. You need people to hold you accountable towards your dreams, people who will push you to be true to yourself.

A lot of us don't realize the impact that negativity, gossip, and drama-filled people have on our lives and our ability to achieve and accomplish our dreams. If you find yourself in a social circle where people are always engaged in drama or unhealthy relationships, or they're caught up in this party life where they always want you there with them and shame you for not showing up, then you have to ask yourself if these are the types of people you really want in your support system. If they are, ask yourself how far they will realistically help you in life if you constantly have to take your attention off the things of higher importance to you in life to focus on conversations and business that don't concern you. We have to really get to a stage where we ask ourselves, "are the people surrounding us the kinds of people we can truly grow and do big things with, or are they people who are constantly going to poison our ambitions?" "Do these people line up with who I'm trying to be in the future and the types of people that I honestly want to be surrounded by?" Take a serious look at your social circle and get real with yourself about whether this is what you want or if you're settling.

As I was growing up and I started to realize I wanted more out of life, one of the first things I had to do was to look at my circle of friends, and when I looked at them, I realized we were on completely different paths, and they had no interest in the path I was headed. When I talked about higher things like living an abundant life and having things that we didn't have at the time, they would look at me and say things like, "here you go again with this philosophical dream bullshit". They didn't realize I was serious, but unlike them, I believed I could have a completely different life in the future. I believed that it wasn't just something we talked about as a way to dream about what we could have, hoping someone would drop us a million dollars, but I genuinely believed I could have it, but they just couldn't see it for themselves or me. So, I had to cut things off and distance myself from them. Our time together was rarely conducive to the kind of growth I was seeking in my personal life. They had little aspirations towards what I saw as possible. When I decided to stop doing drugs, drinking, or gossiping, they didn't even want to hang out with me anymore. When I stopped going to the club, my former friends thought I was acting funny, not realizing that I was simply getting serious about changing my life. It is so important for us to surround ourselves with people who remind us why we should keep going and about what we deserve in our lives. Be around people who push you towards your goals instead of making you feel like your standards and goals are too high. Be around those who will be there for you and support you, and not those who will pressure you into a lifestyle that you don't desire. We have enough people guilting us as it is, so let's not have them in our inner circles.

Don't get me wrong, when I'm talking about your social circle. I'm not just talking about the people who are immediately around you. This isn't about your long-term friends and family members only, but this is also about the new people you allow into your life. Before you take on new friendships, ask yourself how the relationship will help you move in the direction that you're moving in and trying to go in. If you find that someone will be a distraction or liability more than an asset, it's your responsibility to recognize that this isn't a wise connection and refrain from moving forward with building the relationship. You don't have to feel bad for rejecting people into your life. Your job is to only bring in the people who are headed in the same direction as you or can offer something of value that will help you grow as you are on this journey. Before letting go of old friends, it's my suggestion that you have a conversation with them first about what you're doing in life and the changes you're making. Sometimes people in our network are more than willing to accommodate us as we grow - especially if they're growing too. You don't have to cut everyone off and enter completely new relationships. Some people just need to know what you're doing to show up for you, but others will need to be distanced. I used to be so petty and just cut people out of my life over simple things. There were times that I didn't even tell people that I was cutting them off, and I just slowly faded and ghosted some people along the journey who potentially would have been great friends to me. But you know what? We can't go back and change what we've already done, and the only thing we can do is to make better decisions in the future, surrounding ourselves with better people who positively influence us and the things we want to do going forward. We just can't change the past. Another thing that's important to know as we discover our true selves is that everyone is not for us, and we're not for everyone.

Everyone is not for you

So many of us are out here trying to please everyone. We are trying to make sure everyone is happy with us and accepts us. The reality is that everyone is not for us, and there is a strong magic in the art of attracting and repelling people. What this means is that when you're naturally who you are, you will attract a certain group of people who are in line with who you are, and you will also repel people who are not aligned with that. You don't want to try to keep the people who are being repelled. Instead, you want to nurture the people who you attract. These are the ones who see you, understand you, and actually want to be around you. You should nurture those ones because they are the ones who want to see you grow, learn from you, love you, and share their space and time with you. Nurture those people, not to a fault where you're denying yourself, but you nurture them in a healthy manner where you just continue to show up as you are — they will be excited about that. It's when we show up with a mask on and behave like someone that we're not in order to keep people around that we end up being surrounded by people who drain us and constantly make us feel like we're not worthy because we don't meet their standards. Those are the types of people that we WANT to repel and not force them to like us or see us. We want them to unfollow us, we want them to unfriend us, we don't want to be in a relationship with them, and we don't want them to hire us. We should repel them because we shouldn't have to change who we are in order to get people to stick around and accept us when they otherwise wouldn't want us around. When we try to appeal to those we should repel, we give away the capacity we have to put first the things that matter to us, and it takes away our ability to show up for the things that really are important to us.

Understand that you can't please everyone. You can't be everything to everyone, and you don't even want to be everything to everyone because it's draining. It is so natural for us to attract the people who are in alignment with us when we're being our real selves and repel people who aren't our cup of tea. The same way that everyone is not our cup of tea, we're also not everyone's cup of tea. So, we can't expect to become something that we're not just for somebody to stick around us. No! We want people who want to be around us when we are expressing ourselves truthfully in all of our weirdness and craziness, not forcing ourselves to be someone or something we're not in order to make them feel good. We're not in the game of performing and putting on an act for those who cannot appreciate us for who we are and the experience that we bring to the table. It's important to remember that in that repelling and rejection stage, when people say, "no, I don't want to be around you" or "I don't like who you are," we must listen to them because that rejection is protection. Their simple act of rejecting you and not showing up fully for you lets you know that they don't value what you value. They probably don't value you in the way that you need those close to you to value you. They have their own needs and work to do. It's not your responsibility to act like something you aren't in order to make them feel comfortable around you. Everyone doesn't deserve to be comfortable around us because they will try to hijack our lives and stories by forcing us to be who we aren't. As in the case with my former coach, he wanted me to straighten my hair, wear more makeup, only engage with people who had a certain image online, charge "smaller" people high prices to go live with me, separate myself from anyone who was perceived to be "low class", and talk in a way that just didn't resonate with me. I got myself in that position because I ignored the red flags that this was not someone who was aligned with me, and I attempted to fit in with them anyway, and also willingly gave him thousands of dollars to help me curate my business and image. It's like I legitimately signed myself up for the ultimate level of people-pleasing. Every move I made was watched and critiqued heavily. I felt like shit, and I felt like nothing I did was ever good enough, and I soon figured out why. I involved myself with people who did not naturally align with me, and I did not pay attention to the emotions and thoughts I had that screamed — **NOT ALIGNED**. I was trying to show up as someone I wasn't in order to be accepted and approved of to feel important. Meanwhile, I ignored those who were really there for me and didn't require me to perform to be around. Be yourself, and do the things that are true to you. Enjoy your life, live well, be happy, and know that you're not going to die with any regrets because you're taking steps towards living your ideal life NOW. Understand that those who will be there for you will be there, and those who don't will be gone at the first opportunity they have to run. Rejection is your protection, and it keeps you away from people who are really toxic for your future and won't see life the way that you see it. They have different sets of beliefs and views that don't align with yours. Those are people who, if you try to force yourself to fit in with them, will constantly force you to change in order to be approved of by them. They're going to constantly need you to be something that you're not to make them feel comfortable around you, and we're not in the business of doing that anymore, and if we've been doing that — this is it. We're not doing it anymore.

Forgiveness

As you move forward on this journey toward no longer becoming a people-pleaser, it's important to understand the power of forgiveness. It's not just about forgiving others but also about forgiving ourselves. In our past lives, we made a lot of decisions and did a lot of things that, when we look back, we're not proud of or happy about. We wish we would've done something different and knew better, but we have to forgive ourselves because at that time — even if we thought we knew what was right, we didn't, so we did what we knew best, which were the things that were most familiar to us. So, we made decisions based on our set of tools back then and what we were used to at that moment because that was what we were exposed to the most, and that was how people in our environment did things, so we had to look back and forgive ourselves.

I look back at teenage Wini, who got pregnant at thirteen, then again at seventeen and was treated horribly and told that I knew better. I see her and recognize that she didn't know better and didn't have the tools, equipment, and leadership in her life to make better decisions. So, I see her. I see that she had lost her father, who was the person who knew her best while she was in her most impressionable years. Before they could have important talks about life and relationships, she entered a household where she did not have the social and emotional support and care needed to make better decisions going forward. So, I forgive her for not knowing what she didn't know, and I also forgive those who did not know how to parent her properly so that she didn't fall into situations where she was used by men and having sex irresponsibly in hopes that a relationship would fill the hole in her heart that developed when she lost her father. I now recognize that former me, for many years, even into adulthood. I didn't have the tools and knowledge to understand the magnitude of the situations I was engaging in. I now see that I lacked the discernment to realize that everyone did not have my best interest at hand, even when I had theirs. I see her, I forgive her, and I feel for her. She did the best she could with what she had — not knowing that she had options and wasn't powerless to choose better options.

When we know better, we really do better. So, let's extend grace to ourselves for making decisions in the midst of our ignorance. What we did was not a true reflection of who we were meant to be but who we were in relation to the environment and parenting we had at those stages in life. We are all on our own journeys, operating from our own experiences with our own set of tools, and how we express them will be different in the different stages of our lives based on our level of awareness and the world around us. Forgive yourself and forgive others to get right with yourself and continue moving forward. Remember that we shouldn't allow our past mistakes to define us. If I allowed the mistakes I made in my past to define me, I would be stuck big time. I would've never done half of the things that I chose to do in my adulthood, I would've never even had the drive and desire to leave my small country town and find a new way of life, and I wouldn't have even written this book. I would've literally repeated the same things that I saw growing up, but I chose not to. I knew that there was something better in life and that I had an opportunity to make something of myself regardless of what happened in my past. I chose not to hold onto any of the lies because of what happened in my past. Forgiveness is a choice, and we forgive people when we're ready, but you'll find out that the sooner you forgive someone, the easier it is to release. We can't go back and change what happened to us, but we can do our best to ensure that we're not surrounding ourselves with people who are not willing to move away from the past. We also can ensure that we don't repeat those cycles in our own lives.

Affirm yourself and speak life over your vision

It's one thing to have a vision, write it down, and say we'll do it. It's entirely another thing to wake up and say, "I'm going to live like this; this is going to be my reality starting today," and consciously start taking steps now towards becoming who we want to be, talking the way we want to talk, handling conflict in the way that suits our future, and living a life that is truly authentic to us. To become the parents we want to be, the person in relationships that we want to be, and in careers that actually align with us, we have to take steps, initiative, and inspired actions now to make those things our reality. We deserve this, and we have to tell ourselves a different story if we want to become the most authentic version of ourselves who will be happier and no longer need to run away from our present selves because we will be living a life that we can confidently be present in. Instead of thinking that our vision is so far away from us and is a dream that is unattainable in our reality, we have to switch our mindsets and remind ourselves regularly that the lifestyle we want is attainable. Sure, we'll have to do work to make it a reality, and we cannot sit back passively expecting our ideal life to just happen to us, but what we seek is possible. We don't hold the vision in our hearts for no reason, we don't sit around and daydream about the things we'd love to be doing for no reason, and we do those things because that's what we really want to be doing. Now that we recognize that change is in the power of our actions, we must choose better actions starting now. We make adjustments in real time, fighting ourselves and challenging ourselves to avoid hurt whenever things don't work out the way that we want them to work out because we recognize that as long as we're doing our part and being true to ourselves, things will always work out in our favor.

As you move forward in life, it's important to come up with a list of affirmations that remind you daily that this journey you're on is a worthy pursuit and is actually taking you to a place that you have only dreamed of being thus far. Remind yourself that you have the vision in your heart for a reason because it's real. You have the desire to be your true self because it's tied up to the things that will make your life better. Your affirmations are the little guides that keep you on track when things don't work out the way that you think they should. If you want healthy relationships, affirm to yourself that your tribe is out there waiting for you, and if you seek partnership, affirm to yourself that as you grow and become better, that person is also growing and becoming better and at the right time the two of you will meet, and you'll know that you are right for each other. If you want to set better boundaries in your life, affirm to yourself that your wants and needs are important and worthy of being enforced and respected. If you have toxic patterns, affirm to yourself that you can handle tough situations with tact, poise, and grace, listening instead of judging, asking questions instead of making assumptions, and not taking everything so personally.

The goal of affirming to ourselves is to speak things into our lives that push us to change and do something about the situations that we are no longer satisfied with. On this journey to authorship, I had to constantly remind myself that my book was worth writing and that I was a great author if not for everyone, but for those who needed it. This is the kick and push that I needed to sit my ass down in the chair and write, even when it was hard. I had to remind myself through affirmation that writing a book is bringing my vision of becoming a published author to reality, and I'm a creator who can make things that seem hard and out of my reach real. Your affirmations allow you to tap into the future you and ask yourself how they would handle situations. However, they respond to you about how they would handle situations is what you use to write your affirmations and embody what you want in the future now, no longer putting your future off for tomorrow. You already deserve a good life, you already have abundance, you are wealthy and doing the things you want to do in life, you are free and able to make solid choices for yourself, you have a great family, and you handled difficulties well, you speak up for what you believe in and what's important for you, you stand up for yourself when people try to tear you down, and you are already surrounded by people who see you, love you and support you. Affirm to yourself so that you can see what you already have and focus on what's real now instead of what you don't have or what isn't in your life now.

When you have a vision, and there's something you want to do in your life that you don't quite believe in fully, help yourself believe in it by speaking it and affirming it, then move into conscious actions that help you become it. Don't accept any behaviors from yourself that will interfere with what you're doing and who you're trying to be.

Here are a few affirmations that may be helpful for you as you dive into believing in yourself enough to pursue a life that matters to you:

- I really love who I am already.
- I don't need to be anyone else to be worthy of love and respect.
- I have the power to change my life now.
- I'm blessed to live the life I have.
- I'm very wealthy, and I deserve it.
- My blessings are abundant and endless.
- My children are beautiful and creative.
- I've contributed to the awareness of many people even when my life didn't look perfect.
- I'm fantastic at the work I do and choose to do.
- My friends and family are blessed.
- My home is a safe place for our souls to relax and be free.

- I'm cultivating my way to what's right.
- I speak my truth as needed and only the truth.
- My words are powerful, so I use them wisely.
- I'm the creator of my reality, so I create what resonates with me, even if it doesn't resonate with others.
- Healthy love, communication, and relationships surround me.
- The Kingdom of Heaven is already mine.
- My personal beliefs are important.
- I have the freedom to choose infinitely.
- I trust my intuition; it always supports me.
- I'm aware of my needs and the needs of those who surround me.
- I make responsible choices.
- I follow my heart to inner peace and happiness. I forgive myself when I get things wrong.
- I love myself deeply and respect my vision and desires.
- When I've made a mistake, I correct the mistakes that I've made.
- I ask people for forgiveness when I realize I've wronged them.
- I respect people's boundaries. I respect people's beliefs. I respect their values.

Speak life over yourself. Speak truth over yourself. Speak faith over yourself and remind yourself that:

- I can confidently speak up about what I want and how I feel.
- I can confidently and boldly walk as myself.

- I have an open and honest dialogue with myself first and with others.
- I listen to the needs of my children and offer guidance where I can.
- I am honest in my interactions and remind myself that I walk away from things that do not serve me well, Things that seek to hurt me, and things that seek to pull me down.
- I step in closer and lean into those relationships with people who show me their real self and their vulnerability with me, and I get to be vulnerable with them.
- I embrace love, light, and goodness.
- It may not always be easy. But at the end of the day, I still have control and power over my life.
- I have the power and the ability to step away from things that do not align with me and that hurt me.
- I honor my voice and respect my feelings.
- What I need comes easily to me.
- The spirit moves freely through me— the spirit of light and love.
- I'm safe and free to ask for help and ask questions when I'm not clear. It doesn't make me any less human. I am human.

Speak these things over your life constantly and consistently because these affirmations (or those that you create for yourself) will sustain you. And also be willing to accept discomfort because when you're affirming to yourself new things, you're putting in a new code, or you're putting in an anti-virus software, so understand that things are going to be uncomfortable because a lot of these things are going to move against what somebody once told you. A lot of these things are going to directly conflict and contradict some of the stories that you've been told about yourself that have held you hostage and have kept you stuck in one place or that have kept you in the same behavioral patterns that have kept you in a state of victimhood, where you feel like you are powerless in your own right and in your future. So get ready because it's not going to be an easy ride. But it's going to be so worth it.

Recognize that you are responsible for making your dreams/visions a reality

We tend to get so caught up in expecting other people to be the ones to make the change that we need in our lives, but that's not how it works. If we want things to become better, we have to genuinely look at ourselves and ask ourselves, "what is it that we're doing that lands us in the same positions where we are people-pleasing, not getting what we want, feeling unloved, unheard, and unvalued in life like we don't matter." We have to ask ourselves, "what are we contributing to these situations," because we really are responsible in some way, shape, or form for many of the things that are going on in our lives. We are personally responsible for many of our outcomes. So we must perform our part and not expect other people to do our part for us. I've been guilty of this where I expected other people to do all the work for me, and when things didn't turn out how I wanted them to, I was disappointed with the other person. But how can I expect people to do things that will satisfy me when I haven't even done anything to satisfy myself? We can't expect to put the outcomes of our lives into the hands of others and then get mad when it's not going how we want it to. I learned this as a mother who likes things to be cleaned in a certain way. Before I was able to get my children to properly clean our home, I had to get up and do it for myself, showing them how to do it in the way that worked for me.

It's important for us to be responsible for making our dreams and vision a reality. It's important to watch the way we think and feed ourselves with healthy and positive thoughts. We need to make affirmations and speak life into our lives and not get depressed and down even when things aren't working the way that we think they should work. It's our responsibility to say, "ok, this isn't working the way I want it to work, but there are adjustments I can make to find solutions that will help me." It's our responsibility to make our own decisions and take steps toward our goals. If we don't like how something turns out, fine; at least you tried it, and it didn't work for you. Now you're free to try something else that might work better.

Guard your thoughts and watch your behaviors and the way that you speak. What you think becomes what you speak, and if you're constantly speaking disbelief and negativity into your life, then the results of your actions will match that. Be aware of what you're speaking into existence, and make sure it aligns with what you want out of life. When you become aware of who you are and the power of your words, you become able to discern between those who are for you and those who are not in a place where they would add to your life positively.

If you think you can't do something, then you won't be able to do it because you've already said that over yourself, limiting yourself from being able to come up with creative ideas that will push you towards making that thing a reality. At the same time, if you think you can do something, you will open yourself up to new ideas and become creative enough to find ways to succeed and make something happen, even if it seems far off.

Don't live for the external world

One thing that has gotten me in the most trouble and debt has been living for the external world. Trying to prove that you are something to people who don't matter will have you doing things that push you further away from freedom than it draws you in. Think about it. How many people go out and buy expensive homes, cars, clothes, and other material possessions just to appear wealthier than they are? A ton! Just Google, and you'll see that the average American is almost a quarter million dollars in debt - why? Because they want to look like they're closer to millionaire status instead of living within their means and investing their time, energy, and efforts toward true assets. Isn't that ironic? We want so badly to appear to be something we're not for the outside world that we rob ourselves of the freedom we could have to create a life that means something to us. In an effort to impress the outside world, we'll do things that do not make financial sense in order to look like we have financial sense, and it just doesn't make any sense. So, don't live for anyone else because you'll have this image where you look like you have it all together on the outside, but when you open the door to your house, your life, and your mind, it's trashy, nobody's happy, and things are falling apart. We do the same thing with our relationships, where we try so hard to make it seem like things are good on the outside that we settle for behaviors and things that don't make us happy on the inside. The message here is to focus on making sure you're in alignment with yourself and that you are doing things that are truly important to you before you try to show somebody else something or prove something to somebody else.

In 2021 when I first started my business, I was trying to prove that I was somebody important to people. So I was misrepresenting myself where it looked like my business was thriving and doing so much better than it really was, and it looked like my relationships and parenting style were thriving and doing so much better externally, but internally, I was so out of alignment and going into spiritual, emotional and financial debt trying to upkeep it. We have to be careful to avoid getting caught up in this life where we feel like we have to perform or put on an image to impress people at the expense of our own sanity, happiness, freedom, desires, relationships, and health.

We spend so much time concerned with what our life looks like on the outside that we neglect the things that are really important to us. Don't fall for the hype of looking a certain way for the external world. The social media world has really done a lot of us injustice because people show the picture-perfect side of their lives but never really talk about what they had to go through to get it or whether they're even truly happy with it. So we compare ourselves and think other people's life is a standard we have to follow or a standard that we have to live up to, which is just not real in most cases. Don't fall for the commercialized hype. It's most often marketing at a high level, and a lot more people than you know are either in debt but look good, or they're getting paid to flash their lifestyle to you because they get paid when you go out to buy what they're showing. There's a lot of false hype in the world these days where people look like they're living the life, but in reality, they're in massive debt and just another slave to the corporate marketing system. Don't compare yourself to other people, and try to have what they have or do what they're doing because there's no guarantee that they're really doing better than you. Most of the people in our modern society who have no college degree, rent and don't own their place, or live in a semi-run down or old home and drive around in older cars are freer than those who have multiple degrees, own a nice home, and drive around in nice cars — how? Because oftentimes, the person who looks like they're not doing well has little to no debt, whereas the one who looks like they're doing great has a shit ton of debt. Let's be real and honest.

Live your life within your means, and be real about who you are and where you're at in life. You don't have to impress anyone to be worth something or accepted. If you live a less flashy life, celebrate yourself because it will be easier for you to shift your life when you realize you want something more or different. It's harder to shift our lives when we have tied ourselves down in order to impress others. If you don't have a certain level of education, who cares? If you don't walk around in the latest fashion, who cares? If your relationship isn't #relationshipgoals and you and your partner live simply, or you don't have a partner at all, who cares? You don't need to change who you are to be loved and supported and liked. In fact, being yourself will get you much further and will lead to you being surrounded by more important people. Make decisions based on what you want in your future, not what others will think about you.

SECTION 5:

MAKING SHIFT HAPPEN

Making shift happen and really getting into alignment with who you are and the kind of lifestyle you want to live requires you to really do your own work and pay attention to what life is trying to teach you through those uncomfortable moments that keep coming up in your life. Making a shift means you consciously realize that you are the biggest key to your success but also your biggest enemy if you aren't honoring what you really want in life.

Boundaries and Compatibility

To talk more about boundaries, it's important that you have boundaries. As you get out there and take inspired actions based on the life that you really want to live, there will be so many distractions that come your way, and it will be up to you to say "yes" or "no" to them. It will be up to you to either allow yourself to get caught up in the same old same old or push through and believe in your vision and what you're doing for yourself. Will you be able to say "no" to people and opportunities that look good on the outside but just aren't fit for you?

Boundaries determine the kinds of conversations you need to have with people before you let them into your space and your life. So, if you really want to see your ideal life come to pass, you're going to have to set solid boundaries, cut some people off, distance yourself from others, pull some people closer, stop telling yourself lies, and stop allowing anyone to tell you who you are and can be. Think about it, your boundaries are important. If you go to any high-security building, there are boundaries. They have rules for who gets to come in and who doesn't. They have boundaries around the rules that will get someone sent out of their space if they behave in a certain way. Do you have these kinds of rules or boundaries in your life, where there are guidelines for who you allow into your life or guidelines that dictate what actions get people removed from your life? It sounds harsh and a lot, but honestly, our boundaries serve to protect who we are and what we are pursuing in this life. There's a reason why people like Oprah and Beyoncé aren't just accessible to anyone without having to pass a security screening or pay a premium price to be in their presence. They value what they have so much that they are unwilling to just let anyone in their space, and they use boundaries to guard themselves, their possessions, their assets, and their vision from vultures and those who seek to come in and destroy what they've built for themselves. I know many of us haven't reached the level of Oprah and Beyoncé in our life yet, but that doesn't mean we cannot put solid boundaries in place in our life. It's likely that they started putting boundaries around their life way before they became the icons that they are today. They likely started setting their boundaries when they realized they had a vision that was worth protecting.

A good way to start setting better boundaries is by asking better questions that are related to your personality - the real personality that you tend to hide and conceal. Before we agree to a job, relationship, or friendship with people, we've gotta know who we are and what works for us versus what doesn't work for us, then we have to ask people questions based on who we are and what we need from a job, a relationship or a friendship. We also have to keep our future self in mind when we're making decisions, and we have to ask ourselves, "Is this a decision that will help me get closer to who I want to be in the future, or will it push me further away?" We should also ask ourselves, "Is this something that my ideal self would engage in?" Then make decisions from there.

Another thing that's really important on the journey towards becoming ourselves and knowing who we should have around us is compatibility. I personally think compatibility is highly misunderstood and underrated. When we think of compatibility, we typically think of things like do we have the same religious title, the same level of education, are we interested in the same things like where we'll live, whether or not we'll have kids, or whether they believe in the basic things that we believe. We rarely look at compatibility on a deeper level that gauges how we deal with difficult situations, how we talk about other people, or treat those who are different from ourselves. We fail to see compatibility as how well we can show up for others and how they can also show up for us in our ugliness. We may have a friend who says they don't like drama. Even though they may not talk about people directly, they always have something negative to say about the situations they're in, and they also don't want to do anything to move out of that thing.

In my personal life, I realized that I am not compatible with people who sit around and complain all day or make excuses with no intent to do anything about their situations. I'm incompatible with people who look at the world and think it is a horrible place where there are no opportunities, and they're simply stuck in life. I'm not compatible with people who are ok with sharing other people's businesses or talking down on someone or behind someone's back, regardless of if I like the person they're talking about or not. I have a hard time relating with people who cannot hold an intellectual conversation where I can bounce ideas off of them and not just dream about the future but create the future with them. So, in the past, when I was entering certain relationships with people who had those traits, I found myself feeling extremely unsupported and drained around them. I couldn't thrive in that kind of friendship or relationship environment. I learned through former jobs that I didn't want to be in a place that was politically divided, and people who didn't fall in line with the dominant political belief were cast aside. I thrive in places where humans are seen as humans first, and we only address things based on how they're truly keeping us from coexisting and working together toward solving problems in a healthy manner.

Understanding that compatibility is deeper than some of the surface activities you engage in and that it goes into how you do most things in life will really help you move forward. As a thinker, I need to be surrounded by people who will affirm my thoughts but also help me ideate on ways that I can take action. The goal of compatibility isn't to find people who are just like you, but it's to find people who help you operate in your strengths and who are strong enough to fill in the gaps where you are weak. Surround yourself with those who see you and remind you of the things you're amazing at and won't remind you of the things you're weak in. We don't need our weaknesses to be amplified as we are discovering ourselves, we rather need our strengths to be amplified. So involve yourself with those who will amplify you, and you also will amplify them and make one another want to succeed in all areas of your lives and more.

BONUS CHAPTERS:

Here's to transparency. During the process of writing this book, I wrote 3.5 different versions that were similar but very different. I settled on the version that you just read because it was the one that felt most authentic to me, and I feel it would truly serve as a guide to you on this journey toward becoming more of yourself. Once I got to the end of this book, I thought to myself that there were so many valuable things in the other versions that didn't quite make it to this book, so I decided to throw in some bonus chapters. These chapters will continue to help you build on everything that you read and learned in the prior pages, but they may have a slightly different tone to them based on the state of mind I was in when originally writing them. I hope you enjoy these chapters and they continue to inspire you to become more of yourself and less of a people-pleaser.

KNOW THYSELF

Change means nothing if it's done with misaligned intentions, i.e., to prove something to someone else about our worth as opposed to proving to ourselves that we really can be who we desire - simply because we want to and not because we have to prove anything to anyone else. Becoming better just to "show" someone that they were wrong about you is literally people-pleasing. It's like saying, "hey, look at me, look at me, you were wrong about me. I really can do what you said I couldn't. I really am worth something, see". That, my friend, will land you in a tough place if that person or those people continue with their disapproval of you and your way of life AFTER you've made all these changes. Making changes as a way to prove something to anyone other than ourselves is a recipe for feeling even further invalidated, accepted, and approved of than we felt when making that change. To maintain your power and self-control, it's essential that you make changes that are in alignment with what you really want out of this life. You must understand that you are worthy, regardless of if another motherfucker thinks so or not.

To begin making real, lasting changes in your life, ask yourself the following questions:

1. Who do I really want to be, but I'm afraid of the judgment that may follow?

2. What really is the worst thing that can happen if I choose to express myself in the way that is most unique to my desires?

3. What negative thoughts come up when I dream about my ideal future? Is there a positive thought that I can substitute this negative thought with?

There are going to be ample moments along this journey where people will have you questioning yourself and feeling bad for choosing your desires. Choosing to show up differently and really embrace the vision you hold that once seemed like it could only exist in a fantasy almost always causes a purge within our existing social structures — namely those that have been upheld by the masked version of ourselves, i.e., the version of ourselves who changes their voice to fit in and changes their words, bodies, names and our dreams to be more acceptable. It's a facade and a lie. That version is the one that would be unrecognizable if people were able to see into their thoughts, closed-door behaviors, and dreams.

Back in February 2020, I made the decision to investigate the religion of Islam through practice. It was a tough decision because I was literally transitioning from the role of a Christian church girl and group leader to wearing a hijab, 5 Salah praying, Muslim woman who only ate halal and said "Alhamdulillah" for everything. I was honestly excited because I had this deep conviction in me that pulled me toward Islam, and this was one of those convictions that I knew was going to lead me to a deeper understanding of life — even if I didn't know why I was so convicted at the moment. So I did it, and I decided to go for it, telling my friends in the process so that they wouldn't be shocked. Little did I know that this change would lead to people who I thought were close to me dropping out of my life like flies sprayed with raid. I had spent time thoughtfully crafting this letter for my "friends," explaining the change I'd be making, assuring them that this wasn't goodbye, and it was just a "doing something new, so don't be shocked" type of message, but despite my efforts, many of those "friends" cut themselves off from me. Others snuffed at me and told me I was sick and had the devil in me. Some of the women who I thought I was close to walked away from me entirely because they were "afraid to catch" whatever I had, and a few of them tried sticking around, but it felt like they were only there to proselytize me and convince me of all the reasons why I needed to "come back" from this hell bound place that I decided to explore. It hurt, I was sad, I was lonely, and I lived in relative isolation from all my friends for months to collect myself, but I wasn't going to turn around and run back to my former way of living just to be accepted by these so-called friends. Instead, I had to see things for what they were — a blessing. You see, making this change literally showed me who my friends were. It showed me the people who loved me for me and the people who only loved me when it was convenient for them and their agenda. No shade, but I learned that not everyone around me had my best interest at heart, and that was important.

It turns out, when you bet on yourself and make different moves — even if they don't make complete sense to you at the moment — there will be people who disagree and will threaten to leave you, and there will also be people who will leave you, there will also be those who attempt to change you or convince you to go back to your old self so that they feel more comfortable around you, and more importantly, there will be those who show you that regardless of the changes you make they know your character so well and will accept you as you are - even if it doesn't make sense to them. You will also meet new people in the process. Some of them will become good friends, and others will be your friends in transition, meaning that they are only there temporarily to support you during your season of shift. Be careful not to cling too tightly to this new group of friends. If at any time you feel like you are being required to put on yet another facade to be accepted, resist, be yourself, and keep moving towards your true goal. Sometimes the transition is just that, the transition and not the destination. If you ever need to gauge whether you're still in transition, ask yourself these questions, "have I arrived at where I want to be?" "Is this a version of myself that I can comfortably live with long term?" If the answer is yes, congratulations, you did it! However, if the answer is no, keep going — some journeys are a little longer than others. Think of life transitions like a destination that you plug into your GPS. You have an end goal, which is the place that you ultimately want to get to. However, there will be places that you'll want to stop at along the way — some planned, others not. Your job is to remember that despite the pit stops, roadblocks, and detours until you reach the destination that you are ultimately trying to get to, you are not done with your journey. Some of us will be tempted to turn around and go back to where we came from out of fear, and others will NEED to turn around because they'll realize they're only on this journey to please someone else, not because it's where they really want to be.

CHANGE YOUR MIND TO CHANGE YOUR LIFE

I had a coach named Ronne Brown who would always remind us that "mindset is everything".

She used to always say, "Wini, mindset is everything. You are enough, you have everything you need, just flow." I didn't get it, and then I started to study the mind, and I realized, oh my God, Mindset is everything. Many of us don't even understand how important mindset is because we don't understand how our mind works. So, just to give you a little insight briefly into how the mind works, think of the computers that you use; somebody had to install a program for that computer to work for you to be able to access the internet, use Microsoft Office, use your Mac tools, and utilize the basic functions of the computer. Somebody had to install software, the brain of the computer. It involves the way that the computer knows how to go from just a blank screen to the Internet Explorer. The way that the computer connected to the Internet was all based on a software, a program, what someone told it to do, and what someone told it, it could be. Your mind is the same. Your mind is the space where it's almost like software; we have been programmed to believe certain things about ourselves and about the world around us.

We have been programmed to believe in our abilities or lack thereof. Our school systems, our religious systems, our families, and our friends have all downloaded software into their lives. That told us who we could be and shouldn't be, and just like computers, many of us got a virus. What is a virus?

- A virus is something that attacks the system.

- Virus/ venom/ poison - any large group of sub-microscopic infectious agents that have an outside code of protein around RNA or DNA that grows and multiplies.

- Something that poisons the mind or spirit.

- A computer program hidden within another program that reproduces itself and inserts the copies into other programs, and that usually performs a malicious action.

Just like computers, our minds can be corrupted. People with hidden agendas can completely lie to us about who we are and what we're able to do. And if we don't know how to recognize the lies, we'll fall for the virus. If we aren't able to discern, uh oh, there's something here that's going against my belief system, something doesn't feel right, something's off or fail to distinguish between that lie and the truth, and actually bring up a red flag, then there's a high chance that we will fall victim to the virus. The virus then begins to spread and grow rapidly because we don't know, realize and have the ability to detect it. So it just goes unnoticed. Our mind is the same way; every time you do something, and you don't know why you're doing it but you do it anyways because somebody else said you should do it or every time you allow someone to lie to you and you accept that lie even though you know it's not true or every time you say "no" when you know you want to say "yes" or vice versa, you become more and more corrupt. You begin to erode the very fabric of who you were sent to this earth to be. You forget who your Creator made you to be. You forget your own power, and you start to give your power over to somebody else to control you from the outside and take valuable information from you which would completely cloud your judgment and make you think you need other things. They come only to steal from you, to kill and to destroy you.

Your mind is a super computer system. You know what's right or wrong but if you've been accustomed to something wrong in your life for so long, or you've been accustomed to being abused, or you've been accustomed to being afraid to be your real self, then, your mindset will be corrupted. Our minds believe what we feed it and what we tell it. If we are constantly telling our mind that we are stupid multiple times, then that's what we feed it constantly and that is what our mind is going to believe. But when we think, "I am not stupid, what are you talking about? I am brilliant, smart and amazing, I know what's going on, I am aware, and I see", then our minds begin to behave as such.

- It begins to push us into things that are in alignment with that. It keeps us from being afraid of things that we shouldn't be afraid of.

- It triggers us to pay attention when we're in situations or relationships where things are out of alignment.

Our mind is a super computer; you must understand what programming you are allowing into it and whether or not that programming aligns with what you know to be true about yourself and the world around you. You must make sure that programming is one that you can be excited about and happy about having in your life. Mindset is everything; it's how you think, and the thoughts you have about yourself and the world around you. It's good recognizing,

- Are these thoughts healthy for me or are they unhealthy for me?

- Are these thoughts helping me grow and become better or are they keeping me in the same space or making me worse?

When you start to pay attention to your mind and your thoughts, you start to realize how much impact it has over the decisions that you have made in your life. I was in a stage of my life, where I felt like I couldn't get a job with more than a certain amount of money, but guess what? I never got a job making more than a certain amount of money. When I had the mindset that I was unworthy, guess what? I was engaging in unworthy behaviors. I was surrounding myself with people who thought that I was unworthy because they also thought the same thing about themselves.

When I look back and I examine my mindset, I realize that every situation I was in where I was depressed, stressed, or filled with anxiety was because, somehow, I had a thought that played on repeat in my mind and made me feel like whatever situation I was in was all I was worth. My mindset before was why I settled for relationships that weren't for me. When I married my first husband, I was under the impression that I wouldn't find anybody else who cared for me and loved me as much as he did. I was under the impression that I wasn't good enough for anybody else. I was under the impression that he was as good as things got. So I just needed to "fix" things with him in order for life to be better, and it led me to years upon years, from my teenage years to my early 20s, trying to always do something, and just fix myself. I tried to always be the prettier one. Instead of me saying to myself, "there's more out there for you", I constantly tried to convince him of every reason why he shouldn't cheat. I tried to teach him how to treat me. It made me so depressed, stressed, and anxious that there were literally times when I was fainting because I was so overwhelmed. The mindset that nobody else would want me once I had those kids and got those stretch marks and had that broken relationship was what made me continuously take back my ex just because he needed a place to stay or he was in a bad situation. It's the reason why I gave him money so that he could have something to eat and be okay even though he was living with our neighbor who he had cheated on me with. It's the mindset that kept me in a cycle of trying to get him back every time he would go off with somebody else. Because I felt like, "who else is gonna want me with your kids?" I tried everything to keep that man around me. Because in my mind, I had genuinely felt like I was not good enough for anybody else. So I tried everything that I could do to save that dying relationship but it just never worked. So you've got to understand your mind.

Understand your mindset because if you don't, it will lead you into some very uncomfortable positions. If there's anything I learned about the mind it's that when you don't listen to the mind, when you don't walk away from the things that are not serving you, when you continuously try to force something to be that shouldn't be, the mind will always make you very uncomfortable either in your physical body or in your spiritual mental body. You will be in anguish. The real version of you will always try to come through. You will be in a relationship with one person dreaming about something completely different. Once you understand how the mind works, then you become more powerful. Once you understand how programming works, how to be very careful about the types of people that you listen to, what you allow people to tell you about yourself and about people like you, and realize how powerful the mind really is, then there are just some things that you are not going to listen to from people. That doesn't mean that you won't listen to people, but you will be more selective in what you listen to and you will be more selective in what you choose to believe.

I remember working with a lady who just thought that, people like me, weren't capable, horrible at what they did, and weren't smart but rather stupid. This was after I had done a decent level of work in my life and on myself. I remember I used to be really, extremely anxious when I would go up to meet with her. And I wondered why I was so anxious and it was because I had started believing her when she would put herself on a pedestal and put me down. I had started to believe her. Every time we couldn't do something, I started to believe her that I was the one who was failing and not her. She was the CEO, and this was her business so if she knew what she was doing, then it would be fail proof. So I started to believe her that I just didn't know what I was doing, and that I was stupid and less than adequate. I believed that I didn't deserve the job, and it caused me to be anxious every time I was around that woman. But then one day I realized, wait a minute, this was all her opinion, and this was all her own ideology and it doesn't have anything to do with me. This was how she felt about the world around herself. When I realized that, and I paid attention to her behaviors, and to the fact that I was letting myself fall and fall, I said "no, I'm not doing this. I'm not stupid. I'm not a failure. I'm not less than adequate, and I'm not unworthy". And I started to change the way that I spoke to myself. And then from that point on because I spoke life into myself, whenever she spoke death to me from her tongue, I didn't go into those meetings anxious anymore. I rather went into those meetings with power. I understood that I was capable of speaking the truth and I called out things that I was afraid to call up before. For example, I called out the fact that she wanted something to happen in her business but she was unwilling to do it. She wanted to build the business but she was so disconnected from it. She wanted somebody else to completely build it 100% for her without her lifting a finger. And that's not how things work. So I had the ability to show up, and be honest with her about the fact that she's trying to do something that she's not willing to put in the work to do. And it wasn't gonna work and I wasn't going to be her scapegoat. I was not going to be the person that she could point her finger at and blame because I knew that I do my part. I knew that when I know what I'm doing and I know why I'm doing it, it's s*t easy peasy.

But there are so many things that I've noticed now and have started paying attention to and I have this mindset like, oh, this is this person problem. This isn't a "me" problem. It's not that I'm stupid, it's not that I'm dumb, it's not that I don't know what I'm doing but that's just how this person genuinely sees the world. They've put themselves on such a pedestal that anything less than them is dispensable. So I had to remind myself to not be clouded by this. Because if you allow yourself to get clouded by this and you accept these things as true that are coming from this person who has their own problems or from somebody who's not willing to genuinely, really truthfully help you without it being attached to their own agenda then you're setting yourself back. It's almost like allowing that virus into your mind. Allowing the wrong programming to come in and deter and distract you from all that you can be and also keep you from ever going forward and moving forward is troublesome. So you have to pay close attention and understand the power of auto-suggestion. This is a tool that I learned from one of my coaches, Amoya Shante.

What is auto-suggestion? Auto-suggestion is when you replace a toxic thought immediately. Once you realize that what you're thinking about yourself or what you're thinking about in a situation is not headed in the direction that you want it to head in, then you change it. So let me give you an example of what auto suggestion looks like. First, it starts off with throwing out the negative thoughts you have — the debilitating thoughts that you have constantly. Those thoughts tell you you're not good enough, you cannot do something or you can't be someone. You start off by listing those things out. For me back in the day, those thoughts used to be that I was unworthy of a healthy relationship with a good man and I had to replace that with, I am worthy of a healthy relationship with a good man. There is someone out there for me who is going to be the person that I need in my life and I'm going to be the person that they need in their life.

I had to replace the ideology that nobody's going to want me to have all these kids and all these stretch marks with a news story that said; "The man who is going to love me isn't going to be bothered by the fact that I have kids and stretch marks because, he's going to see me for who I am internally. He is going to see who I am on the inside and not just on the outside. He is going to see what I have grown through. He is going to see the real me and not just the facade version — the outside version. He is going to see all this work that I have done. He is going to see how we can come together and be powerful for each other".

I had to also change the narrative that because I don't have a degree, nobody is going to want to buy from my business because

I don't have all these degrees and money and my business isn't just banging and booming; nobody's going to want to do business with me. I had to change that and replace that with, "The people who I am here to serve and I am meant to serve, are going to recognize me. It doesn't matter what condition my business is in because they are going to need what I have and they are going to realize that I have what they need to the point where they realize those things are not of a matter to find to them. They are not coming to me because my business looks great on the outside, but because it's perfect on the inside. They are not coming to me because I am able to put up a bunch of many pictures. My ideal client is not coming to me because my life is perfect or because I went to the perfect school, but they are coming to me because I have been able to master something in my life that they have not been able to master and also because they want to learn to master this thing. They are coming to me because there has been a level of change and growth that I have gone through in my life that even those top schools they went to and even the businesses they were into, were not able to teach them. They are coming to me because I am the person who holds the antidote to whatever ailment it is that they are having in their life at that moment".

I had to change my life around so many things; around the fact that no man was going to want me when I have had all these failed relationships. And I had to say that the right person was going to want me because he understood that there were likely a lot that I had learnt from those failed relationships. And he probably knows that when we have made so many mistakes and we no longer make those mistakes anymore, we are stronger partners because we have had a certain level of experience, and we have run into trouble that we don't want anymore. He's going to recognize that I don't settle for just anything, and I don't just accept anything. He's going to recognize that I am serious and I am not here to play games. I am here for true partnership. I am here to truly be in a relationship with someone I truly love. Someone who we can take care of each other and can raise a healthy happy family together. Someone who doesn't care about having it all or being like the Kim's of the world.

I had to start changing these thoughts I was having: all men are dogs, and all men are just corrupted. Because all men are not dogs, and all men are not corrupted. There are some amazing men out there. There are some fantastic men around me. There are some absolutely great men around me. For me to say that they are all dogs is for me to discount and ignore the ones who are not.

So in conclusion, understand the power of changing the narrative, changing the story, and taking those toxic beliefs that you have, and changing them with what you really want to see in this world. If you think that you're unworthy of wealth, you need to change that thought and that belief and say, "I am worthy of wealth. I'm worthy of having a really great life where I'm happy, where there's an abundance of love, and an abundance of peace, where people respect each other, where people don't talk about each other or gossip about each other, where we don't unhealthily compete with each other, and where we don't have to walk around like fake people. I'm deserving of a life where I have whatever amount of money I want and where I surround myself with whatever it is that I want, regardless of who likes it or not. Even if I want to live small, I can live small and still be wealthy. Even if I'm gonna live large, I can live large and still be wealthy, and not be penny pinching every single day. I don't want a life where I fight to have more, and kill myself just to maintain it and keep it. I don't have to live that kind of life". You've got to tell yourself a different story and you got to understand your future self.

YOU NEED A GAMEPLAN

It's so hard for us to live the life that we want to live, if we don't even know who we want to be in our future, or if we have the wrong idea, or we're trying to be somebody else in our future. So it's extremely important and critically important to really sit down and decide who I want to be going forward? Is my future self somebody who has healthy relationships, happy and always laughing? And is she good with what she has? Or is my future self somebody who's still dealing with all the drama, still being disrespected by men, still being disrespected by so called friends, and still sitting up gossiping, and complaining. Who is my future self? Is she somebody who travels the world and happy and s free? Then her life is filled with love. She's an amazing mother. She admits when she was wrong and she does everything she can to grow and to be better every day. Is future me a victim or a victor?

So map out your future self and try to do it to the best of your ability in a way that is authentic for you. Who the f* do you really want to be? Like really? And don't worry about having it done perfectly. Don't worry about becoming absolutely all that this person isn't right now because as we grow, develop, and learn new things, our future version changes and shifts. The idea of who we are changes and shifts.

So create a future version of yourself that you can honestly feel good about. Create a future version of yourself that if nobody ever knew that you were mapping out this person, they couldn't judge you. Create the future version of yourself that you want to be when you're not worried about money and you're not worried about what people are going to say or think about you. Who is that? If you were living in the middle of absolutely nowhere and all the rest of civilization and society were hundreds of miles away from you, and it was just you in your home, surrounded by only the people that you love. Which people are you surrounded by mostly? And what is your life like? What kinds of things are you doing? What are you building up around you? What's important for you? What do you have? What's your home filled with? And don't worry about this is silly, or this is imaginary. Don't worry about that because sometimes we've got to tap into our imagination to remember who we are.

Sometimes we have to tap back into that part of us that feels like this is unrealistic to accomplish or achieve our goals and to remember who we really want to be. I'll tell you what my future life is like:

- I own a ranch. It is a beautiful ranch. On this ranch I have areas and spaces where I host retreats. My home and all the buildings on my land are made with natural materials. They are healthy not only for humans to live in but for the earth to have to support.

- There are natural water bodies out there, like streams. My grass is good, you can roll around it and it is soft and cool in the summer time.

- I have animals out here, like cows, chicken, horses, and sometimes the snakes come through.

- I have a farm where I grow fruits, veggies, herbs, you name it. I grow things that are healthy for the human body.

My ranch is symbolic of the caretakers of the Earth because the Earth takes care of us. My home is representative of the places that I have travelled all over the world. There's a room dedicated to every area of the world that I have visited and fell in love with. I, a sovereign, I am within my own nation. I'm not within the nation, or under the rule of the nation that does not see me, does not respect me, does not love me, and does not guide me in the proper way. I am rooted in my spirituality and I openly practice my spirituality with my family and I also give my children the ability to choose. I don't force them to practice what I practice, and to think what I want them to think. I allow them the opportunity to think however they want to think and to be whoever they want to be. I allow them to explore life in their unique way. I have an amazing husband who loves being in this ranch. He loves building and creating stuff. He loves being with the animals and just hanging out with them. We are one with nature. People come to my place for healing and they come to be reminded about who they are. They come to be restored and renewed. They come to be rejuvenated, and re-energized so they can go back out to that busy world that can suck you and drain you dry. And they all can function well, they can face the challenges, and they can help make this world a better place in their unique ways. They come to me to receive healing. People from different backgrounds come to my ranch, to my family, and to my farm for healing.

When we're not on our ranch, we have a beach home that we visit. We travel this world, and we go places. We interact with local people of different parts of the world so that we can understand life better. We bring people from different parts of the world to our ranch and to our home so that they can see our world. We take them around, make friends everywhere we go, and build connections everywhere we go in the healthiest of ways.

This is my future self.

- I am a good woman.

- I respect people with differences.

- I respect that everybody has their story.

- I don't hold people to who they once were. Because I understand that we all go through things and we all have the ability to shift and change. But I'm also very conscious and aware of the people that I surround myself with and the impact of being around certain people. So I'm careful about who I allow to get close to me and come into my life.

- I'm discerning and using my intuition to protect myself and family from people who have ill intentions. These people have not yet gotten to a place where they understand life outside of themselves. They don't understand the validity of life that is different from their own.

- I have healthy relationships.

- My mama is doing better.

This is my future self, and who is your future self? How are you living? What are you doing? What kind of life are you building for your family? What kind of things are you building for your kids? I own centers for healing. I own centers that are focused on holistic medicine. I own centers that are focused on native and indigenous community building practices. These are the Healthy kind of practices and not the savage kind that these people have tricked you into believing. These practices are the unified kind where people love each other, have each other's back, protect each other, take care of each other and make sure we could heal and be happy in this life.

What is your future life like? Because, without me having a vision of my future self, it would have been so hard for me to understand how I was supposed to behave in this world. The vision of my future self and the vision of your future self is literally our roadmap. It's what we use to navigate through life in the present moment. It is the thing that tells us the kinds of opportunities we should pursue, and opportunities to say no to. It's the thing that guides and tells us the kind of friends we should have in our lives and the kind of stories and narratives we should accept into our lives. It's the thing that tells us how to invest our time, our money and our energy. It directs us to where we should be going, the types of people we should be surrounding ourselves with and how we should be talking to our children and ourselves. The vision of my future self is the version of me that ultimately impacts my entire journey. Think of this future version of yourself as the GPS you use on your phone or your car when you are travelling . If you just get in your car and you are just going for a ride with no destination, chances are that you are not even using the GPS because you have no destination. You are basically just going, and just rolling with the flow. So you may encounter some crazy bullshit because you didn't prepare for it. If you make discoveries, you make discoveries. You know. But you are still going to get back home, right?

So think of your future version of yourself. You may be saying, "I'm trying to get back home. I've gone too far away. I didn't use my GPS at all. I just kind of hit the road and I just drove for hours and hours. I had no idea where I was going and I didn't even pay attention to the roads I took to get there at all". Whatever the case, think of your future self as the destination you're trying to get to or where you're trying to get back from. For example, you're in the middle of nowhere and you have no idea where you are. You turn on the GPS and you type in your home address. You need to follow the directions that the GPS is giving you in order to get back home. You know that if you take any other turn, there is no guarantee that you are going to get back home. If you just try to make your own way despite what the GPS says, then you're going to throw yourself off track. You're gonna delay your journey and you're gonna put yourself in a riskier position. Our life is the same way. When you finally get that vision of who you are, when you're real about who you want to be, that is the destination. Your journey to get to that person is like the GPS. I know that if my future self is someone who has healthy relationships, then I can't sit around gossiping all day. Gossiping will take me on a detour that can cause me to get lost or to run out of gas.

I know that if in my future, I'm married and in a very beautiful relationship with somebody that wants the life that I want just as much as I do, then I know that I cannot be in a relationship with a man who doesn't even try to fix his own cars. That man doesn't f* fancy the idea of traveling across the world or tending to a farm. He shits on the idea of spirituality in the way that I practice it. He shits on the idea of holistic medicine and indigenous ways of living. I know that I cannot entertain that guy because my guy can enjoys farming. My guy enjoys fixing things. He enjoys getting his hands dirty and figuring things out and spending time with animals. He enjoys those things. He enjoys not being able to spend time in people's faces all the time where he would always be at the fancy restaurants or always at the club. He enjoys not having to do those things. So I cannot put myself in a situation with someone who is because once again, that is a detour. That detour could lead me to a place very far off from where I'm trying to get to.

If I know that I want to become the type of mother that my kids honestly, genuinely and truly feel comfortable coming to, to talk about their problems , ask me for guidance and help them, then I know I'm gonna have to put away a lot of fears and a lot of judgments. I'm also gonna have to check myself on multiple occasions. I cannot be around and surround myself with people who do not believe that children have a voice. I cannot be around people who believe that anytime a child disrespects us, we should just beat them down at the back. I cannot do it. Because of my future self, and the way that I've raised and parented my children, they are not afraid of me. I do not control them. I do not control their thoughts. I do not control their actions. I only serve as a guide to help them make the best decisions that they can for themselves. And when they get things wrong, I do not punish them or abuse them for it. I cannot carry out manipulative, controlling and abusive behaviors towards my children. Because it gets me further away from that vision that I have for myself, and it gets me farther away from the destination that I'm trying to get to. I hope you understand the flow of this and where it's going. I hope you understand the importance of setting a future vision for yourself because you will no longer be lost. You will no longer sit around and accept things and stories from people who cannot see and believe your vision. You are going to have to deconstruct a lot of lies and stories about yourself that you have accepted and believed in your life.

You're gonna have to recognize the trauma as somebody else's trauma that you just so happened to be in the way of and received. You're gonna have to realize that when you feel like you no longer relate to this way of life, or when you feel like this is not who you are, then you can start to remove yourself from the trauma than allowing that trauma to run and rule your life.

I had feared for so long to ask for help because I remember when I was a young girl, whenever I asked for help I would be abused mentally, physically, verbally and emotionally. I remember once I asked my mother for help with my homework, and I genuinely and sincerely needed help with my homework. She went to try and help me but she didn't understand it. She immediately got defensive and went to this place of, "What! Do you think I'm stupid? Like can you figure this out on your own?" I was just treated badly for asking for help with my homework. And it turned out to become a bigger situation that it didn't even have to be. So I didn't want to ask for help. You know, if I made a mistake, then I would get punished for making that mistake. So I couldn't ask for help. I didn't feel safe or comfortable asking for help or admitting my mistakes or asking for help when I needed something because I was always met with this level of ugliness. It made me feel like I was not safe to be in need.

I remember watching how different people talked about others and it just made me feel like I can never get what I wanted because as I listened to these people, they said that people like us don't go off to own things. They said that people like us, you know, these kinds of behaviors and things aren't for us. So I was afraid to go after things because it was like, somewhere there was this unwritten rule that we don't get to be who we want to be. That unwritten rule claimed that we were just forever bound to become someone that a stranger told us we should be. You have to deconstruct a lot of lies. This is the point of what I'm saying right now. You're gonna have to tear down a lot of stories that just don't belong to you. You're gonna have to completely obliterate some of the trauma responses that you've been given. You are gonna have to detach from the judgment that you're afraid of. Remember how I told you the story about me and my Payless shoes. If I were able to detach and deconstruct the lies that I was somehow less than enough because I wear Payless shoes, then that would have never been a problem in my life.

I wouldn't have felt so compelled to go out and spend my money and buy some shoes. Those shoes were very expensive for my liking. I wouldn't have also been so compelled to try and fit in with people who didn't really give a fuck about me and who really didn't like me because I would have understood that they were just living and operating in a lie. That lie says that just because something wasn't made by a specific brand, it somehow makes you less than enough to where you are affiliated with. Now I get it. I get it.

Everything wasn't sourced out in a healthy manner but this wasn't about sourcing in the sweatshops and how things were built. It was about trying to fit in and please a group of people who didn't even understand why they liked something so much and why they hated something else so much. So we've got to deconstruct the lies. We've got to know when to step away from people who tell us that we're not good enough. Do you remember the story about the guy who kept telling me everything was so unladylike? Or the story about the guy almost married, who kept telling me that women don't talk back or go places without their husbands? I had to deconstruct those lies in my life. I had to realize that although that may be true for him, and what he sees and wants out of his future, that was not true for me. That's not the way of life I seek. That's not how I want to do things. I had to move forward from there, understanding that I am enough.

YOU'VE BEEN ENOUGH

If we don't realize that we are enough, if we do not realize that we are already worthy, and if we don't realize that we are already powerful, we will consistently find ourselves settling for people and situations who we expect to be able to tell us who we are. These are the people who we would expect to validate our power and our worthiness in us for us. We will get stuck in this cycle of settling for less, time and time again. Regardless of everything that I've said up until this point in this book, if you don't realize that you are enough, if you don't believe that your beliefs and values are valid, that your vision for life is valid, and that your boundaries are worth setting, then you won't get anywhere. I repeat, if you don't realize how important it is for you to live in your truth, if you don't realize the real version of you is acceptable and okay, then, you won't get anywhere. Everything else is pointless. Because the foundation for everything in your life, to grow and to come to fruition and to be able to see the fruit of what you're looking for, is you understanding that you are enough and because you understand that you enough, then it's easier for you to align with people who also see that same way. When you realize, I deserve the things that

I want in life, and I can believe what I want to believe and it doesn't matter if everyone agrees with me or not then, you have more faith in yourself. Other people have less effect on you. You are much more powerful when you see that you are enough. The reason why it's so easy for many of us to be manipulated and used and abused time and again, is because we don't realize we're enough. We don't believe in ourselves. We have little faith in who we are and who we were created to be.

We have little faith in the validity of the truth that we know deep down inside of ourselves and when your faith is low, it's so easy for someone to come in and give you false hope. It's so easy for someone to come in and tell you what you should believe and who you should be. It's so easy for you to look up to other people based on artificial and materialistic belongings and accumulations and say that person must know something better about life than me. When you do not see yourself as enough, worthy, lovable or likeable, it is so critically easy for you to allow another person to come in and control your life, narrative and story. It will be so easy for you to be like me when I was married to the second guy that changed absolutely everything about myself. If you don't see yourself as enough, you will do everything that they tell you to do and be exactly who they tell you to be and it's so easy for you to lose yourself. Because when you do not see and realize that your identity is your identity, you will give it away for somebody else to create and craft. Giving our identity, our truth and our worth away to another person is one of the worst things we can do because they will extract everything that they can out of us. They will use us in every way that they see possible and when they're done, they will discard us and throw us to the side because they will be over it.

Most people do not seek someone who they can control and just completely mold and manipulate. Most people who are healthy in this world, seek somebody who is on equal terms with them, and who is balanced with them; these folks are who we tend to call in Christianity as being equally yoked with them. That means we hold relatively the same beliefs about life. You are your own person. I'm my own person but when we come together, we're stronger. I'm not completely telling you who you should be and how you should do things. And I'm not completely, you know, putting myself on a pedestal over you as if I'm more important, more meaningful or more worthy. No!! That is the recipe for disaster. So you have to understand that even if you grew up in the worst neighborhoods, or the worst looking families, or you grew up and made lots of mistakes, or your relationships didn't work and you had kids when you were young, without being married, or whatever else requirements they tell us we should meet in order to be worthy or you weren't a virgin when you got married or when you met the love of your life or you didn't go to the top schools or you are not in a top network of people or you don't have this picture perfect life, you have to realize that even in spite of all those things, you are still enough because you are a human, created by God and was put on this earth for a reason. So accept yourself. Accept your story. Accept your testimony, and let go of everything that you've been through. Stop ignoring yourself. Stop lying to yourself. Stop pretending like you are not enough. Stop settling for people who reinforce this belief in you and rather focus on how you can own your truth so in that way you can grow in ways that are meaningful to you. Do not say, "How can I change my truth, or how can I change who I am in order to be more acceptable to other people?" No, no, no. Say, "How can I be more of me? How can I be more accepting of me? How can I be more loving towards me? How can I be more forgiving towards me and even towards the people who once hurt me or once tried to tell me crazy things about myself?"

I want to tell you a story. So when I was 13 years old, I was in a mess. I was grieving. My father had died the year before which was two years before I went from being in his sole custody to living alone in the big city of Minneapolis, Minnesota. I went along in life without having the love of a father. I had a father who really loved me as a child. I went from having the love of my father to no longer having my father and I was completely moved to a different state to Texas, which is my birth state, back with my mother. My mum was also in one of the most toxic relationships ever and we didn't even know each other. So for two years, I had been living with a mother who I really didn't know and we had so much trouble getting along with one another. We had so much trouble respecting one another. I didn't feel safe in her presence. I didn't even feel safe in her home with her boyfriend who was a pervert and just literally a nasty man. And so I searched outside my home to find that love of my father, and to have somebody in my life who really loved me once again because I did not feel loved in the household that I was in. I did not feel cared for in the household I was in. I also did not feel protected in the household I was living in with my mother when I was a young girl. You know that instead of having important conversations with me, my mum and her boyfriend would accuse me of doing things that I hadn't been doing you know. I remember being accused of having sex before I was even having sex and before it became something that was a real and true interest to me. I remember coming home one day and my mom was upset. She asked me questions of my whereabouts and I was so confused. And then we ended up getting into an argument. At the time, I think that I was in my late 12-year-old stage or my early 13-year-old stage. She looked at me and she said that her boyfriend was right. They accused me and said I was going to be just like my then sister in law, who was pregnant at 13 years old and I was so hurt by this because I wondered, "Why are you accusing me of doing stuff? Why are you refusing to believe me when I tell you that I wasn't out doing anything with boys?"

I had a lot of boyfriends and I had a lot of male cousins who were in my age range. We played basketball together, we went riding bikes together and we did stuff that all the pretty girls didn't want to do together. And I also had like a few girlfriends who also did those things too because we were a little bit rough. We were free. I wasn't always interested in just playing with Barbies, and although I did play with Barbies with my friends sometimes, other times, I was interested in more than just playing Barbies. I wanted to go run around. I wanted to play football. I wanted to foot race. I wanted to do those things and the only people who really seemed to enjoy those things were boys. At least the ones that were close to us were guys. So I spent a lot of time playing with guys. Sexually? No. We weren't even kissing each other. We weren't even doing anything sexual. I didn't even have a boyfriend. I had a crush but I didn't even have a boyfriend. So when my mom sat there when I was a young girl and told me that her boyfriend was right and I was going to end up 13 and pregnant, (this was after being accused of doing things with boys multiple times by her boyfriend) I just felt that I might as well go out there and just be having sex. If that's what you're going to accuse me of, then I might as well go out and see what it's like. If you're constantly accusing me of doing that and if you are constantly beating me up physically because you think I'm out there doing stuff when I'm not, then I might as well go and fucking make it happen.

So as a young girl, I went out and I made it happen. I lost my virginity. I ended up getting pregnant at 13 years old. I fulfilled her beliefs about me because I didn't know who I was. I didn't know that there was a different way to go about life and things and that resulted in so many people saying the worst of things about me, calling me some of the worst names ever. They continued threatening me, and gossiping about me around the town. I couldn't even go to school without kids saying things to me and that really took a hit to my self-worth. During those times, I really felt ruined, and then my mom decided to take me to church where they constantly reminded us that if you're not a virgin then you're not good enough and if you've had a baby outside of wedlock, then you're not good enough. So then it reinforced this idea inside of me that now, I really wasn't good enough and I really wasn't worth s*t. So I said to myself, "fuck it, I might as well live fucking wild". Because the church was telling me I was not good enough, the fucking media was telling me that I was not good enough, the town was telling me I was not good enough and my fucking mom was telling me I was not good enough and she was embarrassed about me and other different things.

So I grew up feeling like, "Why the f* should I live a good life? Why should I strive for anything good? I'm already unworthy. I am already not good enough. Look at my past, and look at my history. I've made so many mistakes. I've done so many stupid stuff. I've been out of beds. I was pregnant at 13 years old. Shame on me. Shame, shame, shame. Put your head down. Never look at anybody. Don't ever think that you're anything or can be anybody. Because people like you are trash". That was the narrative I was living with and for the longest time, I thought that I was not enough. Because of that I accepted some bullshit ass people into my life because my self esteem was low and my confidence was low. The belief that I had in myself in me deserving anything good was low because I had been told that people like me did not deserve anything good. But later, I started realizing that I deserve better than this.

I started to think, you know what, this doesn't have to be my story or my life. I don't want this to be the story of my life. I don't want to be someone who has given up hope. I don't want my life to be like all these people who have given up hope. I don't want my life to look like everybody who made a mistake and because they were told that people like you who make these kinds of mistakes are hoes, harlots, adulterers, or fornicators.. I don't want to be like these people who have given up hope in their life and their lives have changed. They're just getting run through by everybody. They've never been able to settle down and find good and healthy love because they've been taught that they shouldn't even believe that it exists for them. They've been taught that they ain't worth it so I said to myself that I didn't want that narrative and that is not how I want to live my life. I decided that fuck it, I exist because I live and breathe. I exist because I have a story and because I have changed and been through all this stuff, I now see the real side of life. I am more than enough to deserve better than this. I'm not fucking dying like this. I'm not dying, believing that I could not have a better life. I'm not dying, living a miserable life where I've given up all hope on myself, my future and my kids. I'm not dying, repeating the same bullshit narrative that says, "Well, we make mistakes". We are our mistakes. F* that and you shouldn't die like that either. You should not allow yourself to live the rest of your life, in poverty, pain and in fear just because someone else who had an impoverished mindset, who was living in pain, and in fear, decided that people like you are not worthy and do not deserve to be anything. At some point, you have to realize that everybody is human, and we're all living these messed up lives, where we think that because we do something so well we're better than other people. I can't tell you how many times in my life I met women who were virgins until they got married and they allowed themselves to put themselves above other women. They said things like, "Oh, I'm so much better than her because I'm a virgin". But when you looked at their life, they were just ridiculous gossips. They were extremely abusive or they had problems in other areas of their life.

When you go around sometimes, you meet people who had the perfect and extremely wealthy family. They got to go to the top schools. They had the best of everything. They've traveled the world. They've done all these things, but then they get back home and they treat their neighbor like shit. They look at somebody next door and they just roll their eyes at them and say, "Poor you. Stupid thing. Dumb thing. Lazy thing." And they're also very critical and judgmental. But some of us have made some mistakes in our life. Yeah, maybe we lost our virginity at an early age, or we got pregnant out of wedlock for the very first time or we looked like we were the talk of the town. But at the end of it all, some of us were still really good to people. We may have been hurt but we were still really good to people. We had our pain, but we were still good to people. So I want you to just look at things like this.

Sometimes, you know, the way that what I like to call our enemy works is that he'll give people this perfect thing in the outside but the inside will be trash. He sometimes throws dirt on the outsides of people whose insides are so pure and so good. He does this to make them look like the trash so that sometimes we aspire to be like people who look good on the outside, but deep down on the inside, they're all trash. We rather look down on ourselves because on the outside, we look like we're paupers. We look like we're peasants. We look like we're poor. We look like we ain't worth the damn things. We look like our mistakes. We look like our past but on the inside, oh God, we are so beautiful. We are so worthy. We are so precious. We are so special. We are so meaningful. We are so kind. We love our neighbors. We treat people with respect. We are slow to judge and quick to help somebody in need and we look at ourselves like we're not enough because when we look on the outside, sometimes it's hard to see what's going on inside. We look at what we don't have, and what we lack and we completely don't see what we truly are. We look at the person down the street, and we want to be like them desperately. They're making us feel bad because we don't have all this money because we're not doing what they do and our body doesn't look like their body. But at night when their door closes, they abuse their family, their husbands, and their kids. They're just mistreating people. Once that door closes and nobody can see them, they change in vile, violent, and gross people. They look at the person on the side of the corner of the street and say, "lazy motherfucker." They would rather throw their food in the trash than take that food and give it to somebody on the corner who is hungry and starving and cold. I must admit there was a time in my life that I was like that too. I looked good on the outside, but on the inside, I was so detached from my life and from my humanity. I was so far away from my true self. But I don't want this to be true for us anymore. We don't need to have this as our truth, where we're so focused on having this Picture Perfect outside, that we forget what it means to be human. We forget that making mistakes is a part of human life. We forget that we should love even if he looks like he's down in the dumps or even if she looks like she's just running around making all the mistakes. We should love our neighbors even if they don't believe in what we believe in, and even if they don't live like how we live. The moral of this is to remember: You are enough. Keep being good, keep being you. Your past? Who gives a damn? We all do stupid shit in our lives. But what makes you unworthy and not enough is to sit around and think that you are unworthy and not enough. What makes you unworthy is when you allow yourself to be inferior to somebody who does not deserve superiority over you because they're not your Creator. If we're humans in this world, we all have equal footing.

DROP THE COMPARISON, YOU ARE UNIQUE FOR A REASON

A lot of us get caught up dissatisfied and living a life that is less than ideal for ourselves because we're so busy comparing ourselves to other people. The only reason why I've wanted all these relationships, wanted certain cars, wanted to work at certain places to get a certain amount of money, and desired to live a certain life that looked a certain way is because I was comparing myself to somebody else. It's because I couldn't see what I had right before me. I couldn't see how precious and special my life was. The only reason I ever really got into any kind of debt is because I was comparing myself to somebody else and telling myself that I want that too. I was going after an image. I was trying to keep up with the Joneses. I was trying to keep up with people on the outside. I was trying to be like other people so I could have this perception of happiness that they had, only to find out that the sh*t sucks; being in debt and being a slave to debt sucks. Being in ridiculous relationships just to have a relationship sucks. Having a business that looks fantastic on the outside but f*g sucks on the inside sucks.

Having a life in general that makes people say, "Wow you just look so happy and you look so great" sucks. Walking around with a facade and a mask on and not being able to be myself or be able to say, "Okay, I don't want what you want", sucks. It sucks. It's horrible. It's the number one way that we mistreat ourselves. It's a very horrible way to treat ourselves.

End the comparison. Stop looking at what you don't have in life and looking at what somebody else has whiles coveting that and changing your life around to have what they have. Stop trying to be like someone else so that you can be accepted by other people. Chances are the people that are not accepting you because you don't have a certain look or a certain background, are still not going to accept you. They may accept you temporarily, but they're still not going to accept you permanently.

I'll talk briefly about changing my religion. When I changed my religion, I tried to be a part of a group of people who were more accepting of the fact that women who had children and were single moms, still deserved to have love and be in relationship with men. I wanted to be a part of a group that had that kind of mindset.

I wanted to be a part of a group that emphasized that we're forgiven and they didn't just emphasize that in theory or word, but in action and behavior. I wanted to be a part of a group where I felt like I belonged and where I felt like all my past mistakes could be dissolved and I could just be me again. And when I found this group, I realized that oh my God, in order to be acceptable, I'm gonna have to be perfect. I'm gonna have to talk about how I read my Quran every single day. I'm gonna have to say all of my salah regularly, every single day. I will even have to do the extra salahat night. I'm gonna have to attend all the halaqas. I'm gonna have to attend all the khutbahs. I'm gonna have to talk about how I am at every single Jumah service, how I don't listen to music anymore, how I was saved from music, how I was saved from dancing and how I was saved from those unbelieving friends. I tried to get into this group of people and then I realized, oh my God, like they accept me now. I'm able to perform, and I'm able to come in there and just share all the stories of the good things that happened to me. You know, we don't talk about any of the other stuff; we just pretend like the past never happened. We only talk about the good stuff and we just strive to be excellent. And I have nothing against it. But I soon came to understand that thinking that another group was religiously better for me, just because they made it look better on the outside, did not mean that the group was better. So I joined this group of people. And you know, I surrendered my old way of life. I was actually pretty mean to my kids at the time, which is what nobody knew. I forced my kids to say the prayers with me and if they got the prayers and the words wrong, I got angry and upset with them because I was told that if you don't know how to do this and say the things in the Arabic language, then, you know, you're really not having a real connection with God. And you know, all I wanted to do is to have a real connection with God. But it became performative, right? And how did I get myself in that situation? I got myself in that situation because I looked at Muslim women in my circle and in my network, and they just seemed so perfect.

They were covered. You know, a lot of them boasted about keeping their virginity until they got married. So I was coveting their lifestyle and I thought that they were better than me. So what did I do? I started shifting and changing myself, and becoming more like them in order to feel better about myself. I started comparing myself to the little Christian girl that I was in my Christian group. I started comparing that and saying, "Well, this one looks better."

So let me go over there and get this one. I soon realized that it's all the same shit just a different level.

The first time, you know I was a speaker. I had a platform that they had given me, where I went on and I spoke regularly about different topics and conversations, you know, relative to my shift and my change and how life was going now that I had gone from being an unbeliever to a believer. And all it took was the one time when I decided to show my real self. I had on my hijab, I had on my dress and my boots and I was fully covered but I decided one day that I just wanted to go out so I went out to this really cool IT place. It was late at night, dark and I turned the music up; not the lights to my car. There was this song playing; it was called 'single as fuck'. I really liked that song, so I turned the music up. I turned on my camera, and put it on my dash. I got out of my car, and I started dancing to the song by myself, just out by myself because I was single as fuck and I was just moving and grooving. It wasn't like I was getting knocked down and dirty. You know, I'm saying that even though I could have if I wanted to, I was just moving and grooving and doing some interpretive dancing to 'single as f*' by Foushee. And I thought oh my God, I felt so free. I danced because I was literally for the first time in my life single and I was cool; I was good and I was alright with it. I started to realize that all these women who I had prided because they were so accepting, so embracing, and so loving, had taken all that love from me. And they essentially told me that if you didn't take these things down especially the video that I posted of myself, dancing to this horrible, horrible music then I was not going to be able to be a part of their platform. They didn't say it like that. But that was the insinuation you know; they had this lady who was running these things. She would call me up and ask me, "Hey Wini, we saw the video that you put up. Is there's something wrong with you? Like we think you need to take it down." And I was like, "Oh, there's nothing wrong with it. I was just having some fun. I'm gonna leave it up." So I left it up and then I ended up going to videography class at the gym, where choreography is the way that we do the exercise right so I'm in my workout pants. I've got my long sleeve shirt on. I've got my hijab on and our dance instructor was teaching us how to do the body yody yody yody dance, you know. And so here we were, shaking our juices and our jellies and exercising, and I had recorded it because I wanted people to see and say, "Hey, here's a different way that you can get some exercise in and like actually have fun while doing it." But then once again, I received that call that said, "Wini, we think your videos are inappropriate," and then I received another message that said that the panel that I was on for an upcoming conversation, no longer needed me. When I asked them why, they were reluctant to give me an answer. So I said, "Okay, that's fine. I know what it's all about." I knew it was about the fact that I was dancing and because this group of people thought women don't dance. Good women don't listen to music like that. Good women don't do what you're doing.

I got canceled. Right? So here I am; ungrateful for the life that I have, coveting another person's life, comparing myself to another group of women, and shifting myself to go and fit in with this other group of women just to find myself once again canceled. I was canceled by the Muslim women, and canceled by the Christian women because I was too spiritual, free and I had different beliefs than them. Because I was willing to practice and learn other things, I was canceled by the Christian woman who told me that I was sick, and told me that you know, it must be the devil in me or something like that. I was canceled by the Muslim women because I wasn't perfect since I listened to music. I was canceled because I went out and did something that didn't represent them well and what they were trying to portray about their perfection right. So, I found myself in this situation again, where it was like, "Wow, like what's going on here?" I think once you find a group of people who say we accept you, we love people as they are, we know that we all have mistakes and we don't hold our pasts against us, then there's like these, other layers that are always underneath it. These secret layers say, but if you want to be with us, you got to be like this, or you got to behave like that. And I've never been a sucker for just behaving like somebody just because. I've always wanted to be around a group of people where I could just be myself. It was clear that I couldn't be myself around these people. Yet again I was comparing, shifting and changing myself to fit in with a group of people who at the end of the day, when I actually behaved as my real self, they didn't want me around or they were threatening me that if I didn't change things, I wouldn't be able to hang out with them and I wouldn't be friends with them or anything like that.

All these happened because I was so ungrateful for the reality that I was enough as it is. Because I was so busy comparing myself to other people thinking that they were somehow much better than me because they kept themselves covered, talked a certain way, walked a certain way, and did certain things, I yet again allowed myself to fall, and to be defined by a group, not myself. I pushed myself further away from who it is, that I was, and what it was that I was trying to do in life. I had allowed myself to become a little bit less of myself to be accepted. And as soon as I felt comfortable enough to be myself, it was like, ooops, sorry, we don't like you like that. So, don't compare yourself to other people. Don't feel like you have to be someone else in order to be accepted. Don't feel like you got to talk a different way, walk a different way, look a different way or have different things in order to be accepted. Because what I'm going to tell you is that no matter what you do, if you're doing anything to be more accepted by people other than yourself, then chances are there's gonna come a time when those people will see the real you and then decide and say no, you're not acceptable. So you have to accept yourself first. Stop comparing yourself to other people and accept yourself first. Accept yourself as you are you girl; you are a big bum, big body, big juice, girl. So accept yourself as you are and stop trying to be like skinny girls over there. Okay because you have no idea what's going on in the mindset of that skinny girl over there.

You are living small while everybody else around you is living large. Okay, accept yourself like that and understand that just because you're living small and everybody else is living large, it doesn't mean that you can't be yourself. Be yourself anyways. Because that's your truth. That's who you are right now. And unless you want to change it honestly, and you're going to do it in a way that's not going to sacrifice your sanity and your freedom, then I would just be okay with, this is who I am, and this is my level right now. We got to know our level and we got to stop trying to get stuff just because other people have it or just because other people make it look good. You know that grass saying which says that, "the grass ain't always greener on the other side?" And they say some people use turf grass or excuse me, sometimes the grass is greener, but you get over there and you realize that this is turf grass, and it ain't even real grass. You get over there and you realize, damn their grass is way greater than mine but this is all fake. And underneath it is some f*g barren a*s land. They are not actually growing sh*t over here. This land ain't fertile over here. It's just covered up and it looks good. My grass may not always be green and during different seasons, some might become brown or some might have little patches mixed with it. But one thing I can say is that my grass is real. My grass is my grass and my grass was a reflection of how well I was taking care of it or the seasons that we were in. So stop looking across the fence. Stop looking at your neighbor and saying, "Whoa, what do they have? How do I get that?"

Start looking at what you have and how you can take better care of what you have. Study how you can take better care of who you are. Because you will be unhappy time and time again. You will find yourself in shitty situations time and time again. When you think that what somebody else has is better than what you have (don't get me wrong, sometimes people do have something better than what you have), instead of going in trying to get what they have, you should actually go sit down with them and ask them how they got it, instead of trying to duplicate it without any understanding and knowledge about how they even got it, or what it's even made of. You need to go have a conversation with them and say, "Hey, I noticed your grass is like really green. Can you tell me more about what you do to keep it green? Like what are some ways that you water it? You know, I noticed that you're in good physical health. You know, how do you take care of your body? How do you eat? What are some of the things you do? I noticed that you have this really lovely house and this family that always looks happy so how are you making this happen?" Ask people, and inquire; because sometimes you're gonna find out that the way that people have stuff either requires you to do some different work, or it requires you to do things differently. If you don't ask the necessary questions, you might rely on, "Oh, oh, you had to manipulate a lot of people to get what you got? Oh, you lied to people to get what you got? Okay, okay, you did? Okay, this is not real. It's fake. Oh, are y'all really mad at each other? Do y'all really hate each other when you are inside the house?" Like you realize everything is not what it seems when you actually go and have a conversation with people.

Sometimes things are great. They're great because that person was putting in some ridiculous amount of work to maintain it. Sometimes things are great because that person is concealing what is really going on, on the other side. So instead of comparing yourself and just saying that based on the outside appearance of things, I want to be like this person or I want to have what this person has, or I want this thing to be going on in my life so that I can feel like I'm good enough to them (because I keep comparing myself or somebody keeps comparing me to them), go and figure out what makes that person look good, and what makes you like them so much. Are you willing to do the things that are required in order to get there? Do they even live align with what you want in your life? Because there are some people out there who their wives are happy because they get paid off for everything. They pull out money out of their wazoo in order to keep their wives mouths shut about the abuse, cheating, lies and mistreatment of their family and themselves. Because the money is sufficient for them, they're willing to keep the money and shut their mouths and not even say anything. They don't complain at all about the abuse because they value that material life so much. So you have to be very, very, very careful.

You know, if we look at the Kim's of the world, everybody wants to look like them. They say things like, "I want her life. I want her body, I want this. I want that." It's like if you really open things up, those types of women with that caricature figure are usually not as happy as you think they are. And the proof is in the pudding. It's in the way that they talk and in the way that they treat people. It's in how much they're able to love themselves as they are. Like if you constantly always need a new surgery, do you think you're really happy? And I'm talking about cosmetic surgeries. I'm not talking about, the surgeries that actually fix something because it's broken or not working. But I'm talking about you're constantly getting lip injections, constantly getting facial reconstruction, constantly getting liposuction, or whatever it is to keep your body looking good. What does that say about our mind? What does it tell us about our mental state? There's something off in our minds where we cannot accept what we actually look like. We don't feel good with what we actually look like. If that's your thing, do it. I'm not saying don't do it. If it's your thing and if it's genuinely your thing, okay you can do it, but if you're doing it because you see other people doing it, and because you think that by doing that, they made their life better, then you might be in for a rude awakening. It's because all that change and all the things that you're seeking, lives within yourself already. And the change is inside your mind. It's not in how well you can duplicate another person in doing what they're doing. By no means whatsoever. That's not where change is. That's not where change lives. That's not where change exists. Okay? At all. So before you start trying to upgrade your life and change your life, to be like somebody else who you perceive to be better than you are or more worthy than you, you might want to check their records. Ask them to open up that record book. What kind of stuff are you going through right now? What kind of stuff did you have to go through to get to where you're at? And then you have got to really, really, really look at yourself and say am I willing to go through those things? Am I willing to ignore my mental health needs? Am I willing to consistently cheat people or manipulate people or mistreat people in order to have the things that I want? Am I willing to put in all the work that is required for me to change my internal self in order to really get the things that I need?

The next thing is we've got to start learning from our past, and not only learning from our past, but learning new things in general. It's hard to grow. When we're operating from a limited perspective, limited information and limited knowledge, it's hard to understand that there are people out there for you who are going to be healthy for you and willing to grow with you. They are people who are willing to be a part of your tribe. I am going to use my country town as a reference to explain what it means to operate from limited knowledge and limited exposure If all that I would have known my entire life was this little country town that I had grown up in, and I had never ventured out of that space and engaged with people who were drastically different from myself, then, I would still be in this mindset even though deep down inside I knew I was different and I knew that I wanted more. I would have still been in this place in my life. I would have thoughts like, "I'm the one who is obviously wrong. There's a problem with me because I want something different which I believe are different things from these people, but because this is all that I know, they must be right and I must be the one that's wrong."

You know, if we're not surrounding ourselves with other things, getting out of our environments, taking trips to different parts of the States, different parts of our city, and different parts of our world, we would be limited to what we thought actually really existed around us. You know, I grew up in a space that didn't have access to a lot of beautiful green trails and a lot of creeks that were clear and you know, it was quiet. Although we had those things around us, it wasn't as easy to access them. I didn't really know how to access those things. I grew up in a place where you didn't really see black people in roles of power or influence. You didn't really see them as the mayors of the city. You didn't see them as doctors, lawyers, or as people who held certain positions that were different. You know, you only see them in relatively few spaces and limited scopes. And, when you see people in limited scopes and limited spaces, it kind of makes you think that there's really nothing else out there for you. Right? You don't really believe that you can do anything different for yourself. So you have to get into new places. You've got to go and explore. You've got to get around people who have a different religious belief than you. You've got to get around people who have different lifestyles, different home styles, different educational backgrounds, and a different upbringing than you. This is how we learn and this is how we grow. This is how we expand our mind. This is how we break out of the limitations that have been set up around us.

We break out by seeing something different. I think one of the things that really helped me as a child was the fact that my dad went to war. He was in Vietnam, and he went to different countries. He was in the military. He traveled a lot and it seemed like he's seen different things. He had seen different ways of people, and he would sometimes take us to the little Vietnamese shops, and to the Asian food markets. His best friend was Indian, so we got to be around Indian people too. He eventually put us in a school where it was extremely diverse. And we were also in an immigrant community where literally the majority of the kids came from families that had migrated to the United States of America. So they were First generation Americans and so through the interactions that we had, and the lessons we learnt about the different systems, the different ways of lives, and the different family structures, there was a significant impact in our lives because we realized that whoa, what we have been given is really not the only way. And it really doesn't make us superior to other people. So learn something different, and get outside of the box. Step outside of the limited knowledge that you have been given. Step outside of the assumptions and the prejudgments and go figure something out for yourself by engaging and interacting with people who are different from you. I Instead of trying to force them to accept what you believe, listen to them and hear what they believe. And remember, you don't have to change your beliefs just because somebody else's beliefs are different. But you can allow the differences to be something that make you think more, open your mind and realize that God's green earth is very diverse. And it's filled with different ways to worship Him, and filled with different ways to love one another, respect one another and to come together and build.

So go learn something new. Educate yourself. Network. Get out of your comfort zone. Be willing to be the dumbest person in the room. Okay? Because through that, you learn so much. You have the ability to learn so much. But make sure that whatever you put yourself into, aligns with the future that you want to see. Okay? So don't go around and just accept that anything is true, just because it's happening outside of yourself. Go into things while still believing in yourself. You shouldn't feel like you have to hide yourself when you're in these spaces. Go into these things owning it; own who you are and don't repeat the mistakes of your past. Reflect on what went wrong in your past. I am where I am today because I reflect a lot. I spend a lot of time introspecting. I spend a lot of time looking at myself and saying okay, what did I do to end up in this situation? I spend a lot of time thinking through something I've gone through that I found to be unpleasant and not aligned with my future. I spend a lot of time saying, "Okay, well what do I need to do different going forward?" I spend a lot of time literally asking myself. At which point did I allow a narrative or belief that didn't belong to me, take over? Where did I spend too much time trying to please somebody else in order to feel like I was worthy? How did I get into these situations that I did not like that and that ultimately were not for me? And what can I do going forward to ensure that I don't continue to make the same mistake?

For me, in my dating life, since this is where I've had a lot of learning lessons, I had to realize that I was pretending to be somebody else. Anytime I went on a date, I would hide my real self. I would try to be this perfect girl. I would try to show up as you know, brainless. I would try to show up as like, innocent and all these other things that I thought were gonna make somebody love me or appreciate me or respect me or want me more. You know? I said to myself, "Let's talk with our proper voice. Let's be really good. Let's go along with what he wants to do. Let's pretend like I don't cuss you know because if he doesn't like cussing, then I'm not going to cuss. Let's pretend like I don't sometimes smoke a little weed because I do sometimes smoke a little weed but I'm going to pretend like I don't and if he says he doesn't like it or if he says it's something that he's not, you know, like a behavior that women shouldn't do, then I'll stop it. I won't do it again." So I entered these relationships with this complaint facade, where I was ready to completely change just in order to keep a guy and it was consistently putting me in a situation where I was with people who weren't the people I want to be with because I was living a lie. The version of me that's with them is not what I really am. And when I'm doing things that I want to do, I got to hide, right? But you know, if I listen to trap music, and he was somebody who didn't listen to trap music, you know, I would pretend like oh, I don't listen to trap music. Then I would get in my car and be on my way home and I will be jamming the f* out. We'll get into the importance of filling your mind with the proper stuff a little bit later. I will pretend like I don't smoke and all this stuff and then I have moments later where I'm sitting on my balcony, but he's not around me and I'm rolling up a jig. And I had a completely different side of me. There was a completely different version of me. From the perspective of this guy who I was dating, I wasn't a smoker. It was like, what do you really think is gonna happen if you guys ever move in together and live together? It's gonna be catastrophic. Because you're gonna start being that version of you even though he clearly told you that he doesn't like people like this who do these things and then he ain't gonna want to be around you anymore. Because it's like, you're not the person that you presented yourself as. We do not want to do that. Learn from your past. I figured out what it was that allowed me to get that job that I knew I was overqualified for. I figured out what allowed me to stay in the situation with a toxic boss who was micro aggressive all the time, and always put me down to feel better about themselves. I figured out what allowed me to be in that situation?

Was it desperation? Was it fear of not being good enough? Was it fear of this being the best that I could do? What was it? Learn from your past. Look at those relationships. Look at the jobs, the situation, and the lifestyle choices that you made, that did not work, and really sit down and be honest with yourself about what part you played in it. A lot of the time, we like to be the victim. We like to be the one who when we look back, we are like we had no part in that; that was just a horrible person, or a horrible boss, and this is a ridiculous situation. They did all these to me. They did all that to me. But we rarely like to look at ourselves and say, "Damn, I was really BS* myself. My self-esteem was really low. And I got into it because my self-esteem was really low." We rarely like to look at ourselves and then tell the truth about ourselves about what we personally did in order to land ourselves in that situation. We don't talk about how we tried to become suddenly perfect. We don't talk about how we started doing things that we didn't do before jus to please this person to keep them around. We don't talk about how we were willing to just sacrifice amazing parts of ourselves just to fit in and be approved of and to feel accepted or feel like we're worth something. We've got to start looking at that.

As a parent, I was full of sh*t. And when I look back at my past life I'm like, "Why were you full of sh*t?" Well, I was full of s*it to my kids because I was so busy trying to hold up all these other images on the outside. Let's just be real with ourselves. What behaviors and what patterns are you doing? What decisions are you making? What beliefs are you holding on to that are constantly leaving you in a place of feeling stuck or feeling like you're not worthy or feeling like you can't go on and actually live the life that you want to live and do the things that you want to do? As we move forward, we have to really start prioritizing ourselves. We have to realize like I said before that, it's not going to be perfect and we're not just going to change overnight from who we are today and all of our bullshit into the version of ourselves that we want to be. It is a journey. And it's a journey of self discovery. It's a journey of recognizing where we're falling and it's a journey of also recognizing where we're thriving, recognizing what we're really good and recognizing the things that we really want to be doing and letting go of anything that doesn't align with that even if it's uncomfortable. It's a journey of really leaning into those uncomfortable moments where we have to change our behavior, where we have to show a side of ourselves that we were afraid to show people, and where we have to say, look, I've been kind of fake, I haven't been real with y'all and I've been making things seem like they're all good but they ain't and I'm tired of it.

Because all this fakeness is not attracting the people that I really want around me. It's attracting people who are cool with me when I'm in my fake a* stage, but as soon as I become myself y'all run off and I don't want that anymore. I just want to be real. So that way real people can come and be around me. I just want to stop this bullshit. I just want to stop playing these games and more than anything, I want to be in alignment. Yeah. I don't want to have to hide or feel like I'm hiding. I no longer want to be around people who are going to get up and cancel me just because I'm dancing, or people who are gonna get up and cancel me and unfriend me and not want to be around me just because I'm studying or practicing or investigating a new religion, a different religion, and a different way of connecting with God. I don't want to be around people anymore who only like me when I can do something for them. I don't even want to be around myself anymore when I'm being dishonest with myself about my needs or when I'm saying yes to things that I don't want to say yes to. I don't want it.

You've got to prioritize yourself. The only way you're going to be able to live a life where you're no longer accepting people's bullshit is when you begin to prioritize yourself. When you begin to say, you know what, this is my truth and if it makes you uncomfortable, then I'm sorry because there's nothing about that I can do for you. Maybe you need to go figure out your truth so that you're not so uncomfortable with other people's truth. Get to a place where you say, "Look, these are my boundaries and if you can't respect them, I cannot allow you into my life no matter how good you treat me and no matter how much you might give me or do for me or be around me. If you cannot respect my boundaries, I cannot give you my time and my energy. If you're mad at me, criticizing me, calling me names and talking bad about me behind my back just because I'm moving differently then I'm sorry, and like deal with that on your own. But don't expect me to change who I really am. Don't expect me to f*g flake out on myself or sell out on myself anymore in order to please you. F* pleasing anybody. Let me please myself. Let me please my Creator. And I'm sorry if you don't think the same way about the Creator as I do. Then, that's on you. Okay, great. So practice your religion, practice your spirituality, and live life how you want to live. I'm sorry if my parenting style isn't similar to yours. That's cool. Great. As long as I know that my parenting looks like how I want it to look and it's fitting my future vision for how I want to be able to show up for my kids, that's cool with me! Parent how you parent. But don't expect me to change the way that I parent and be mean, or rude, or horrible to my kids or be this overly pushover for my kids, completely acting out of fear of all the things that might happen. Don't expect me to do those things just because that's what you do. Like, I respect what you do. So respect what I do, and if you can't respect what I do, just get the f* out of my way. Really. Don't come around here because I don't need another fair-weather friend. Like I don't need another person in my life who is only going to like me when I'm performing up to their own standards and oftentimes standards that they themselves can't even live up to."

Something that's important as we shift and change and start to become more of ourselves is planning our reactions ahead of time. Because like I said, people are going to be uncomfortable with our change. People are going to be uncomfortable, when we start showing up as our real self. That version of ourselves who says no, when we usually said yes. People are gonna be uncomfortable with that. People aren't gonna like that. There's gonna be a lot of people around you who were enjoying the benefit of you when you had no boundaries. But now that you got boundaries, they can't have their way with you. They can't get over on you with bullshit stuff that they usually were able to get over with you initially.

It's like, you're gonna have to say you know what, if I'm in a relationship with a guy and he's making it very clear, that he doesn't want anything serious with me or he's not looking towards the future that I'm looking forward to, then I'm gonna have to sit down with him. And I'm gonna have to say, "Hey, we can't do this." And if he begs and pleads and says, "You know what, like, I'll get my shit together. I'll think about it. I'll work it out. Give me some years, and some time to really get myself together." You have to be ready to say, I'm sorry, I can't do this. And then you have to allow yourself the space to grieve because it is literally an act of loss even though that person isn't dying. It's an act of loss when we have to cut ourselves off from or let go of people or situations that no longer match with us and we were really hoping they would match with us.

I did the same thing for jobs. When I realized that it was time to get up and quit my job, it meant it was time to have a difficult conversation with the boss, instead of being afraid of what was gonna happen or if they fired me. What's gonna happen if they don't want to hear me? If they're gonna fire me, then look, let me just make sure I prepare myself. Let me save my money, so I can have my bills covered, and make sure I pay my bills ahead. You know, let me make sure I start, getting my resume together. Let me maybe start getting my business together if a business owner is what I want to be. Let me make sure that I'm setting up my life to be ready for the event that if I'm gonna be fired, (this is something we should already be doing), then I should already be like taking care of myself and preparing for anything in the future. We should stay stocked up, and we should make sure that our bills are paid in advance. We should make sure that we create a safety net or an emergency backup plan for ourselves in any situation because you could get sick and that can come between you and your job. You know, so just prepare yourself for that situation. And then also prepare yourself to hear them push back and say, "No, I think you're wrong. I don't think this is what you are saying." I think it's damn what you're thinking but prepare yourself and don't be so overly emotionally reactive when they do say something like that to you. You know, try to not fall apart but say, "Okay, it's just what it is. We're obviously not aligned. It is what it is. This is it. That's all. It's not working. We have two different beliefs about what things should be like. Okay, great."

Let's start planning something different. This is something that I did in real life. When I realized that me and my teammates that I had been working on a project with were not going to be good teammates to go long term, and I couldn't give them what they were looking for, (because what they were looking for really wasn't anything I could get to begin with) and we were never gonna see eye to eye and things just did not align between us, I said, "Okay, great. But here's what's gonna happen going forward. I'm going to help you get a new team. And when you form a new team, I'm fully exiting because I cannot be here and because this is not healthy for me. I'm not gonna be able help you build your business. You need to get somebody who's here, and who's gonna be able to help you do those things."

So it's like we got to prepare ourselves for those tough conversations. We've got to prepare ourselves to be met with family members who are dissatisfied with us and who are unhappy with us when they realize, oh, you don't follow the religion of the family, or oh, you're okay with a completely different lifestyle that we were never exposed to or we were taught is bad even though it has no harmful effects on them or anybody else. You have to prepare yourself for that. What you might find is that sometimes things go a lot better than you think they will. Sometimes people don't even realize that they're causing you any kind of trouble or pain. So when you talk about it and when you have those difficult conversations with them, then they say, "oh my God, I didn't even realize that! Oh, shit, I'm so sorry. Like let's work on this." That is if people are genuinely willing to work on it with you.

But either way it's best to start planning your reactions ahead. So that way, you can be grounded and you can remember who you are in an emotional situation. That's difficult.

You need to have difficult conversations. You have to prioritize your truth. Okay. You have to speak your own truth. I know speaking our truth can be hard especially if we came from backgrounds that were abusive, where speaking our truth could lead to physical, mental or emotional or financial abuse. I know it can be difficult. I know it can be hard. But we still have to do it. We still need to do it. It's still important for us to do it and it's still essential for us to do it. Our truth is critically important because that is what guides us through this life. It is what ensures that we move in the proper direction and that we don't settle for things that are not for us. It's what keeps us out of situations that serve as detours and roadblocks and prevents us from getting lost in the direction that we're headed in.

Next, we're going to talk about affirming things to ourselves. We talked a little bit about auto- suggestion, and about replacing some of those negative thoughts we have with positive thoughts. But now let's talk about affirmations. Let's talk about installing a new software into our minds, changing our belief system and giving ourselves a new belief system to operate in because after all, regardless of what you tell your brain, your brain is going to listen and it's going to believe it. You can tell your brain complete lies and your brain is going to believe the lies and then it's going to start to help you live a life that is in accordance with those lies. Or you could even tell your brain a new story. It may not necessarily be true for you right now but you can tell your brain this new story. And then guess what happens? Your brain starts to work to make that your reality. Your mind starts to work to make these things your reality. It starts to work to make the story and the narrative that you're assessing into your life your reality and your truth. So, we're going to talk about affirmations and really crafting affirmations that are going to help you grow forward in your future. So it's time to flip on to the next chapter.

FEEL WHAT YOU FEEL & KEEP MOVING FORWARD

I know we live in the age where everybody is telling us to get out of our feelings, and completely ignore our emotions. But sometimes we need to lean in to those emotions and those feelings in order to understand what's really going on with us. We don't give those people the power over us because sometimes we'll feel fearful. That doesn't mean we must allow that fear to stop us from heading to where we're going. But it rather means that we should feel that feeling and allow ourselves to feel it. Don't beat yourself up, don't ignore yourself and don't numb yourself because the feeling comes up. Acknowledge the feeling that you're afraid right now. Acknowledge that you're scared.

Throughout the course of writing this book you're reading right now, there were many times when I was so afraid. I thought to myself, "What if I write this book and nobody reads it? What if nobody buys it and nobody learns from it? What if people go on a sh*t campaign and just, you know, completely put bullshit under it?" I was afraid and for a moment, I wasn't writing like I needed to. I could barely get past the first 3000 words of this book. I could barely move past the first chapter of this book because I allowed fear to get to me. But then, I leaned into that emotion and I said, well why am I afraid? And that's how I discovered all the things I said like, "Well, I'm afraid because I don't want to be a flop. I don't want to feel like a failure." And I asked myself, why are we so attached to feeling like a failure? This book is our truth; this book is my truth. This book outlines a lot of what I did in order to grow, change, and go from being a violent person who hated life, herself, and wanted to die. I changed from someone who was constantly drunk and drugged in order to get by and feel good about herself. This is my story. This is my truth. These are the things that I really did in real life to come out of some of the ugliest situations of mine. It doesn't matter if people like it or not. It doesn't matter if people are going to shit on it and disagree with it because they have the right to do that. They have the right to say that this isn't going to work for them. That doesn't mean that it's any less valuable and that also doesn't mean that I'm any less valuable. So I had to really fill into that emotion of being afraid and fearful. I had to really sit down and connect with my emotions and how I feel, in order to get through that moment and get to the other side. Well now here I am. We're so deep into this book. I'm not gonna give up. I'm not stopping. I'm gonna continue to pursue my goals and you have this book in your hand now because I said, "Even though I'm afraid, even though there's parts of me, that are fearful because I'm going to be embarrassed and even though things aren't gonna work out with this book, I'm still gonna write it because it's still valuable. And even if it touches just one person or two people or a handful of people, I have done my job. And that's all I need to worry about doing, as it is my job. Because as in the words of my amazing coach, Meka Miller, who has been supporting me while I was writing this book, and has been helping me work through my fears, she said, "There are people who need you and most importantly you have something to prove to yourself." And I was like, "You're right. That's it. I'm not finishing this book because I want all the accolades. I'm not finishing this book because I need 50 million people to approve of me, accept me, and make me feel good about myself, but I'm finishing this book because there is somebody who my journey and the tools that I used to make it through some of the difficult parts of my life are going to help them. I'm putting this book out there because I've wanted to do this. Because since I was a teenager, I knew I wanted to write my story out since I was 17 years old, so I started to realize that I had a story about what I went through that people needed to hear. I just knew I wanted to write.

First of all, this book is about the healing that I went through that I can now transfer to somebody else. And secondly, it's about showing my 17-year-old self that she wasn't wrong. It's proving to her that she was right when she said we have a story. We have a testimony. It's proving to her that we don't have to be stuck and tied to our past, and we don't have to be afraid of what people are gonna say and think. It's proving to her that we did this baby, and we had the faith. So that 17-year-old planted the seed and I carried it out later in my older years. So I checked in with that fear. There were some times when, I was incredibly sad, going through these stories, deeply in tune with the ugly side of my emotions. There were times when I was building my business that I felt incredibly embarrassed for always coming online and selling my services at the standard price and not even making many sales. I was embarrassed and I had to lean in to my emotions and say why am I embarrassed? Oh, I'm embarrassed because in my first year of business, I didn't gain a million dollars. I'm embarrassed because in my first year of business, I didn't even hit 100,000. I'm embarrassed because in my first year of business, I only served a handful of clients. I only served a few people on a one on one basis and a few people in groups. I was embarrassed because I thought that I was going to get out there and just grow my business quickly. I didn't realize that this was a journey that was step by step and that I needed to make sure I got clear on my path. So it was really embarrassing for me so I leaned into that embarrassment. It took me a while but I leaned into that embarrassment. I had to remind myself that, honey, you have literally helped people through your services.

Through your business, people who have actually paid you to help them and you helped them to the point where they literally talk about how their families are a thousand times better or to the point where they literally talk about how their mindset and their thinking is way better or to where they're able to go out there and live their dreams, then they're able to go out there and start doing the things that are important to them. They no longer beat themselves up the way that they've been beating up themselves. And it's like, that point is more powerful than jumping into business in the first year and just making a whole bunch of money and not being able to serve people. You know, I look back at that embarrassment and I say well, what if a bunch of clients came my way? I would just be drained. It took a lot of energy for me to serve the clients that I was serving on a full-time basis. How was I going to handle 1000s of people that it was going to require me to work with, in order to get to millions of dollars? How was I going to do that? I was going to be drained and then people were going to get half a* work from me. And they probably were not going to get the quality level of healing and attention that they needed from me as their coach. So I had to lean into that embarrassment and then I had to ask myself, "Why are we so embarrassed? Oh because we want things to look a certain way." And I had to check myself and say you know what, maybe it wasn't what I thought it was gonna be but I was able to help people and I learned a ton about myself and a ton about business in the process. I learned so much about what's more important than being able to hit financial figures. I learned that helping a family grow and shift which meant helping a wife, a son or daughter, a mother or a husband, or other people in a relationship, bond together and become healthier in society, was more important than just jumping out there and seeing all the numbers shoot up right away. I would have been extremely overwhelmed if I couldn't give quality service to people. Now, this isn't to say that this is not a goal of mine because they are still goals of mine. But as I look back at myself when I was in those embarrassed stages, where I quit on myself, where I stopped my business because I felt unworthy and I felt like nothing that was supposed to go away was going away I remind myself that, "You are worthy. This is a part of the journey. This is a part of the lesson." This is a part of seeing, if you are really committed to doing this work that you say you're doing, even when shit is ugly. Even when it's failing, or even when it looks like it's not working because you're looking at the wrong things. Feel your feelings, okay? You're changing your life. You're becoming the version of yourself that you've always wanted to be in a society that tells you shouldn't desire to be the person that you want to be. That's not easy. It's a challenge. It's difficult. You're gonna have different feelings come up, and you're gonna grieve. You're gonna have moments where you're sad. You're gonna have moments where you start losing hope. You can lose faith. You're gonna have moments where you doubt yourself. You're gonna have moments where you're afraid. You're gonna have moments where you don't want to walk away because you're used to the feeling of things. But all I ask you while you're feeling your feelings is that you don't succumb to your feelings. Don't let your feelings overwhelm you and lead you to making decisions that are going to be out of alignment with who you're trying to become. Instead, lean into those feelings. Examine why you're feeling that way and reaffirm yourself. We talked about affirmations earlier. Make affirmations to yourself. It's okay to have feelings that are not always the happiest and bubbliest feelings out there. It's okay to have moments where you're upset and angry because maybe things aren't going the way you want them to go. It's okay to have feelings where you want to give up. But it's also okay to acknowledge that you know what, even though I feel this way, this doesn't necessarily mean this is what I'm doing or this is where I'm at. Even though I might be afraid or a little angry right now, I don't have to stay here. And I don't have to make a decision based on this emotion. When you are overly emotional or when you are in a mood where you have to make a big change, be slow to make decisions based on your feelings. Be slow to make decisions based on, your anger or your sadness or your fear. Be slow to make decisions even though you feel excited. Let me tell you how my feelings have manipulated me in the past.

They were tons of moments where people were able to manipulate my emotions, okay? They were able to say things like, "You know, you are a single mom and you live in this lifestyle. You just want to live better. You want to have better, and you want to do better." All these things affected me and sometimes my feelings got so caught up. Anyways, you are right; I am a single mum yeah, yeah, and I really want some money. Yeah, yeah. I really want to do things different in life. Yeah, yeah, yeah. Sometimes, I would get so excited about this person that they had the solution to my problem, that I would just go and spend all my money with them just to realize that they were just really good at highlighting my pain points. I would sometimes make a decision based on the fact that I was feeling like this person knew me so well. They knew what I needed so well that, I could just give them my money. But I must tell you that before you make decisions based on your feelings, you need to sit with yourself, and investigate. And if you're making a big decision, like buying a house or buying a car, entering a relationship, leaving a relationship or getting a new job, before you just accept something and make a decision based on how you feel in that moment, you need to really sit down and ask yourself, does this decision that I'm about to make really align with who I am showing up as and who I want to be? Just because this job is offering me more money than I've ever had in my entire life (and I'm excited about having more money than I've ever had in my entire life), does that mean that this job aligns with what I really need? I can be excited and make a decision that's not good for me.

Just because I am scared to leave this relationship because I'm afraid that when I'm out there by myself, I'm not going to be able to sustain myself or I'm going to be broke or I'm going to be lonely or any number of things, that doesn't mean I need to decide to stay with this person. I need to think through things before I make a decision, regardless if my feelings are all the way up or all the way down or in between. I need to take time to say, "Okay, I'm feeling this way right now. But just because I'm feeling this way, it doesn't mean that I need to take a certain action. For example, just because I'm embarrassed because my business is not performing as well as I expected it to perform in the first year, that doesn't mean I should quit. It doesn't mean that I'm invaluable. It doesn't mean that whatever I'm offering to the world is useless. It doesn't mean that at all. Just because I'm excited because this person seems to get me, understand me and know me because of the things that they're saying, doesn't mean I need to take the decision to join their program or give them all of my money. No, instead I need to sit back and I need to investigate. I need to go and I need to look through their stuff. I need to see and ask myself, are they somebody that future me would be proud to say that I was in network with that person or I worked with that person or I engaged with that person? Am I in alignment with their business model? Am I in alignment with the way that they treat other people? You've got to look at those things because as I was excited and super souped up and happy to work with some people, I eventually gave a lot of money to people who when I looked at how they treated others and how they talked about people behind closed doors, I was like, "Wow, who did I give my money to? I was so happy to work with this person but oh my God, this is not ideal for me." So listen, feel your feelings but do not allow your feelings to control your decisions. Do not also make decisions based on your feelings. Instead, sit down, check in with yourself and make sure that after doing some research, this is what you want to do. Okay? It's important, to not confuse our feelings and our intuition. Okay?

There's a difference between discernment and how you feel okay? Discernment is like this level of knowing. It's when you're able to say, "I've seen this before and I did not like the outcome of this. So let me proceed with caution or let me take my time to really look at the facts." On the other hand, your feelings don't always care about the facts. Okay? So you have to be careful with your feelings because they do not always care about the facts.

Something else that's really important as you go on this journey of changing and growing and shifting is to pause often to pray and to meditate. Those affirmations are similar to prayers. But pause often before you react to people. Pause and ask yourself, "How do I want to react to this situation?" Pause and ask yourself, "Do I even want to engage in this conversation?" Meditate for a moment. Take a deep breath in and breathe out. And do that multiple times until you can restore your balance and you can think clearly again. Tell them, "I'm sorry, I can't give this to you right now. But give me a moment to sit with myself and think things through and I'll get back to you." If they can't respect it, then I don't know what to say for them. They're gonna have to respect it and you're gonna need to set that boundary that says, "I'm sorry, I know you want to talk about this right now. But I can't talk about this right now because I'm not in my right state of mind and I don't have the answer that you're looking for at this moment." I remember trying to force a guy that I was talking to, to engage in a conversation with me that he just didn't want to have. Like, I wanted him to answer things. I would tell him you know what you're looking for, you know what you want, and you know all of this. And he just wasn't in the mood to have that conversation. I was trying to force him to do it but it just made things worse. Because at that time he didn't feel safe, and he wanted to take his time before responding. I also at that time didn't trust him and it was because I was not being patient. Sometimes people are gonna have to be patient with you and you're gonna have to teach them how to be patient with you. Okay? And then other times, you're gonna have to know like, when to just speak up and tell the truth but pause often, and say, "Give me a minute to think about that." Pray and say, "God, Creator of the universe, and angels. Higher Self; Show me the way. Be with me and guide me. Forgive me when I get it wrong. Show me the right way." Also meditate. Take time every day to just be thankful for what you have. Appreciate the sun on your skin, appreciate the birds in the sky, appreciate the trees, grass and the fact that you have people who love you and the fact that you have shelter in an environment that you're safe in. And if those things aren't true for you, meditate on what you can do next. What can I do to get me out of this situation and get me out of this environment? More importantly, ask for help when you need help.

You're going to need people and if you have people around you who you cannot have or help you safely and confidently, then those are not going to be the people that need to be closest to you. If you have people around you who are going to make you feel bad when you're in need, then they're not the people that you need to surround yourself with. So surround yourself with people who are okay with helping you. Surround yourself with people who support you and who see you. Surround yourself with people who are going to tell you the truth and not something else that is manipulative because they seek to gain something from you. We don't want people around us who are fake friends. We don't want people around us who are just going to tell us what we want to hear. No, that's not what we want. At all. Leave it, don't bring it our way. No thanks.

It's challenging to grow your support network and get around people who are really going to help you. It takes breaking traumatic cycles, especially for those of us who I think I may have mentioned this before. We are the people who have been taught that asking for help makes us weak or somehow less than enough, and it keeps breaking our mindset. Growing your network requires stepping into new friendships and walking away from some old ones. It's not easy because it's a challenge. But you've got to trust yourself. You've got to be honest with yourself and what you need. You got to expect that things are not going to be immediately exactly what you're looking for. It's going to be a process of trial and error but just trust that you really do know what's best for you. Even when you make mistakes, just know that you still know what's best going forward. And if you do feel like you are just really, unable to do what you need to do, to get the help that you need, to have the confidence, to have the faith, to have the relationships, and to have the conversations, then sometimes you're gonna have to invest and pay somebody to help you. You're gonna have to come out of your pocket and say, "Hey, I need a therapist. Hey, I need a coach. Hey, I need a mentor. Hey, I need somebody who can sit here and help me write my resume. Hey, I need somebody who can sit here and help me make sense of the shit that I've gone through. Hey, I need somebody who can train me. I need somebody who can offer me new tools." Sometimes you got to pay for your support network and that's uncomfortable for many of us. We're afraid to pay for our support network. We're basically afraid to pay people. Yeah, you're gonna pay some people and your money is gonna go down the drain but you're still gonna learn something from it. So it's not going to be in vain. You're going to learn to pay more attention, be more present, and be more aware in the decisions that you make and the things that you do. So, the right people can really help you move forward and get to where you're going and you can start wading through the wrong people.

CHANGED BEHAVIORS ARE THE ONLY THINGS THAT LEAD TO CHANGED OUTCOMES

——————

Acknowledge your own BS patterns. Know thyself. Look at the dumb shit that you do. Change your outdated beliefs, behaviors and patterns.

I grew up in a family where on one side corporal punishment, AKA a whooping with a belt, which involves beating your kids whenever they didn't listen to you or they did something that you didn't like, was normal. I grew up in a family where I didn't have the ability to speak up and say my part to defend myself or to say what I wanted or to speak to my mother and actually be heard. She would always tell me, "You're the child and I'm the adult so what I say goes. Period!" There was no debating it. There was no arguing about it. There was no challenging it at all. And a lot of people where I grew up in the small town had the same mindset, where it was like, "Oh, your mom just said something and you just told her she was lying or she was wrong, so you deserve a beating." Even if she was really lying or wrong, your mom just told you to do something that you didn't want to do and you had the nerve to say I don't want to do that. You deserve a beating. And it was normal to be beaten over stuff that didn't even make sense. It was normal to be beaten for just asking silly questions. I remember when I was a kid and I asked the question, "What are those!" as I was pointing to either one of my sisters or my cousin's boobs. And I was like, "What are those?" Because they were different boobs. My mom had well-developed full-blown boobs, and they had these little things that was like they didn't really look like they were boobs. They were boobs or something else and I didn't have that. So I wanted to know genuinely as a kid. What are those? Do you know that I got beat for asking that? I got beat. I was told not to ask that stupid question. And when I asked why because I really wanted to know, I got in trouble.

And then, as I became an adult and had kids of my own, I started repeating those same things. You know, my kids make a small mistake, and here I am ready to whoop some a*s. My kids wanted to talk back to me and here I am ready to whoop some ass. They wanted to yell at me and say you're not listening, and I wanted to whoop some a*s. Why the f* am I supposed to listen to you? You are a child. Because those were the patterns that I had been consistent with, and that I had instilled in me as a child. It was instilled in me that I needed to control people outside of myself, instead of controlling myself. So I repeated those same behaviors, and those same patterns; whooping my kids if they did something wrong, instead of sitting down and having a conversation with them. So I had to get real and honest with myself that look, you are the problem. This is a human being. They have a perspective, and they have an opinion so why don't you sit down and hear them out and actually explain things to them, instead of just saying because I'm the adult you have the right in beating them, when they inquire further. Why don't you sit down and actually have a real conversation with them and guide them so that they get it? All they're seeking is to understand why certain things are happening. They're new to this world. These are kids, and they're still learning about how things work around them. I had to check myself and realize that oh shit, all my kids want to do in some cases is defend themselves. They want to speak their piece. They want to say what was going on in their opinion. All they want to do is to have some say in their punishment. All they want to do is to understand why things are the way that they are. If I tell them, you're grounded, and they ask why, it's because they genuinely want to know why. If I tell them to do something, and they ask why, it's because they genuinely want to know why they should do it. And it's my responsibility as the parent to not get angry and upset and assume that they should know better. It's my responsibility as a parent to help them know better and to actually teach them and sit with them. It's my responsibility to treat them as though they were another adult sitting next to me asking me why.

In my relationships, it was the same thing. I thought it was okay to be hitting on people, and fighting people. Anytime I got mad at them or anytime they didn't want to talk to me or give me an answer that was satisfactory to me, I had to realize that I was the problem here. I didn't realize it even in my business, and even in the things that I was doing. I expected people to just do everything for me and I didn't have to do anything. And then I realized my business wasn't thriving because I expected everybody to do my business for me whiles I do nothing. I was not willing to put in the work for the parts that were important. I realized that some of my friendships were shitty because I was unwilling to speak up and say the truth because I was so afraid that they were not gonna want to be friends with me anymore. That was a me thing. I was doing the BS*. I was the one doing the bullshit. I was the one who consistently had the negative relationships because I wasn't doing my due diligence. I consistently got into relationships with people who didn't align with my future. But it was my fault because I kept changing myself, expecting someone to love me for me. How the f* can they love you for you when you are changing who you are? They don't even know you. So we have to be real about our bullshit behaviors. Sometimes as parents, we ignore the fuck out of our kids. We tell them everything they should do, and everything they should be. We compare them to other people, then we wonder why they're so f*g jacked up. We wonder why they rebel. It's because we are not listening to them. We don't give a f* about what they have to say. We're not there for them. We just want to dominate. We just want them to cooperate. We want to f*g dictate everything that they do. We think we know what's best for them when they really do know what's best for themselves in many cases. We assume that they don't know what's right when you're the one who had to teach them what's right. This f*g small system is teaching them what's right from wrong. The school systems are teaching them what they want to teach them based on the agenda that they have for them going forward. We got to look at our own bullshit and ask ourselves where the fuck we are we bullshitting ourselves. Why are we expecting people to understand things when we've never sat down and talked to them about it? Why are we expecting people to treat us a certain way that we've never even taught them? Why are we expecting people to read our minds and to just know things like out of the blue, without us ever having to sit down and talk to them through these things? Why are we expecting people to change their behaviors just because I have an opinion and I think that my opinion matters more than theirs.

How am I expecting this guy to suddenly want me and tell me that he doesn't know if he wants to be with somebody who has kids? How can I expect it if I have just been really great and really nice, treating him very well. He's gonna suddenly want me? Why am I expecting people to change their behavior for me? I need to be real with myself. I'm not even acknowledging with myself that look, you cannot expect people to give you what you're not going to give yourself. You cannot expect people to be something for you when you're not there for yourself. You want somebody that can wife you up and tells you he doesn't know if he wants kids. He's telling you that he doesn't even know if he wants to be in a relationship right now. And you want him to just suddenly become somebody who's ready for a relationship, just because it's you?"

He's telling you that you are not right for him. How do you expect him to change and listen to you when you're not even listening? You're perpetuating this bullshit behavior, where you expect people to suddenly want you and suddenly do things for you because you're going above and beyond. You say things like, "I'm going to show you why you need to be with me. I'm going to give you all the sex that you need. I'm going to buy you nice things. I'm going to do sweet things for you so that you will want me." But he's saying things like, "No, I don't want to use these things for me. I'm going to enjoy them by the end of the day. I'm still not gonna want you. You're still not the person that I'm looking for. I still don't want you. I'm not connected with you on that level." Next stop is I'm here busting my ass and doing everything. And then I cry like I did with the ex-boyfriend I told you about. Oh, I changed myself to become everything and more for him. And then I was stuck looking stupid when that wasn't enough. But it was like, he had been telling me. He had been telling me the kind of woman he wanted in his life. He had been telling me that he didn't want to live with me. He had been telling me that I was not the person he wants to be with long term, and I was not the kind of woman who he wants to introduce to his family. His family was not going to be accepting of me. He had been telling me all these things. But because he was still giving me his time and his energy, and still accepting my gifts me, taking him anywhere he wanted to go, feeding him, having sex with him, he had no incentive to go anywhere else until he found that other person. But it was foolish of me to think that I could do something to change somebody's mind. What I should have done was to say, "Okay, it's very clear that you and I do not belong together. Here! Be released. Go hang out with somebody else. Go enjoy your time with another woman. I'm gonna go find what I'm really looking for without you."

We have to look at our own behaviors and stop bullshitting ourselves. We have to stop pretending like the whole world owes us something. We have to stop pretending like everybody needs to change for us. No, we need to change for ourselves. We are the ones who have to start doing something. We are the ones who have to stop doing the bullshit. If we want our lives to change, we have to be the one to change it. We can't expect everybody else on the outside to change it for us. That's a big, big, big mistake and it's only going to leave us unhappy and dissatisfied. That's all it's gonna leave us with. We have got to forgive ourselves. It's important to forgive ourselves. Once we move out of this phase and once we realize that we've been doing a lot of bullshit and that we've been the ones who have been responsible for all the outcomes in our lives and in our adult years because we really can't blame our teenage years on anybody else because we were under the guidance of somebody else, we start to interact with the world in a new way. We have to own the fact that you know what, it's my responsibility to change my behaviors and if I haven't changed my behaviors, all these outcomes are my outcomes. They're my burden. They're things that I brought upon myself because I didn't go out there and learn what I needed to learn. You may say that you have not started changing yourself in the way that you need to change but that's not true. Because if you read this book, that means you are somebody and if you're this far into the book, that means you are somebody who is actively seeking to change. You are somebody who wants to grow and you are done with the bullshit. You are done playing yourself. You are done getting into these crappy a*s relationships and thinking that the person should change in order to suit you. You're done with the jobs that don't align with your future self. You're ready to start saying, "You know what, this is who I really am. This is what I really want and I'm not taking anything if it ain't it." You have to become responsible for yourself. But when you notice that you have been bullshitting yourself, don't beat yourself up. Don't kick yourself. You've been down for a minute, honey. You've been down and you've been held under by generational curses. You've been held under by the trauma and the poor parenting that you received when you were growing up. You've been held down by other people's ignorance. You've been held down by a system and society that is trying to make you feel like you're not anything so that way you don't receive the blessing that's there for you.

So forgive yourself because we don't know what we don't know. Forgive yourself because we were ignorant and didn't see any other options. When the models in our lives have been people who have settled for bullshit ass jobs, where they're barely making any money, have shitty benefits, don't get to spend time with their kids, and working around like slaves, we go and repeat that same thing. We can't beat ourselves up because we did what we had seen. When we get into these toxic a*s relationships with these men who don't give a f* about us, and our kids, and they don't treat us well, and we also stick with this ship for far too long, we can't beat ourselves up because that's what we grew up seeing. We saw our mothers or our fathers in crappy ass relationships, treating people like shit. We are a product of our upbringing. But that does not mean we have to remain stuck in that situation and that does not mean that we have to beat ourselves up and not allow ourselves to grow and not allow ourselves to progress because of that. No, we get to say, "You know what self, I forgive you. Because you had what you had. You knew what you knew and back then the tools that you were equipped with were some bullshit a*s tools. I forgive you and I forgive everybody around me who didn't understand what they were doing because they were just doing what the generation before them did." That's what a curse is. A curse is repeating the behaviors that consistently just kill you and keep you in a state of servitude and slavery. So we need to forgive ourselves, and then we must give ourselves permission to grow. We must give ourselves permission to be a victor to say now that, I know how the game is played. I may have lost back then, I may have taken a bunch of Ls, but now that I know how the game is played for real, I'm about to come to this bitch and win even if I lose.

Be patient, and trust the process. Okay? Meet new people. Learn new things. Fill your mind with information that builds you up and doesn't tear you down. Be careful of the music that you listen to. Be careful of the people that you follow on social media. Be careful of the podcast that you listen to. Be careful of the things that you read on Google because everybody has their own agendas and some people's agendas are vile. If you don't realize that, you will read something and let somebody make you feel less than yourself. If you want to know whether or not something's good for you, I'll tell you, this is the test right here. Things that are good for you build you up, even when they hurt. Okay? So, for example, if I'm out here running wild in the streets, cussing people out, firing people, and somebody comes to me and says, "You know what, you are really mean. You have really hurt a lot of people. You are really being disrespectful to yourself and others and that makes me feel like shit." But at the end of it, I come to the realization that oh my God, like I've been a crappy person? Then that's something that builds me up. It may not feel the best, but it's something that shows me the truth so I can actually see myself, okay? But if it's something that's telling me that I should continue to be this vile person, or tells me that I'm worthless because of these vile actions, or I'm trash, or I'm undeserving because women like me, don't get anything then that's the kind of shit that you need to throw away. Throw it away because that is meant to continue to destroy you. It's meant to instill a level of fear in you, and it's meant to rob you of your faith. It's meant to keep you in the cycle of allowing the wrong people into your life. So if you want to know if something's right for you or wrong for you, gauge; does it make me better at the end of it? Am I a better person as a result? Am I making better decisions in my life as a result? Or am I continuing to make poor decisions and continue to beat myself up and continue to bring myself down? Okay? Pay attention. Let all your blessings be your blessings. Okay?

Let them be the things that help you change the narrative and break the curses to change your future, change the way that you treat your children, change the way that you treat the people in your relationships and change the way that you treat yourself. Let all of these lessons in these encounters that you've had that have been uncomfortable, be the things that guide you towards getting what you actually want. Getting what you actually desire is going to fulfill you and satisfy you. Let all these be the reason why you become even more of yourself, so that way you can get rid of all the people who don't belong in your life, instead of settling for them. Let these be the reasons why you stand strong on your convictions and why you stand strong on your faith and belief that you really can get what you want. Because you know that when you start to shake on that and allow other people to tell you what to do, then that's when sh*t really f*s up. But we don't want that in our life anymore. Become somebody that you would love to be around. We talked about changing the narrative. But now it's time to change yourself. Step up, implement, take action, and do things differently. Ask yourself anytime you're in a situation where you're like, "Oh, we don't know what to do about this" that what the fuck will my future self do about this? MY future self who's a boss bitch. She's a bad bitch. She's out there doing everything that she needs to do. She doesn't let people step on her. She stands firm in her faith. She stands firm in her convictions. She believes in what God has for her. She believes in her abilities. She believes in her talent. She believes in her strength. What would she say about this? What would she do? That's what you think about because you are her and she is you.

Become who you would love to be around. These are the people that you admire, and the people that you respect. Don't forget that you admire and respect them because that is something that is already in you. You admire and respect them because, they are a reflection of a part of you that you've been wanting to show but you don't know how to. So now all you do is to become that person. Say you know what? I really love being around people who speak their truth and let me speak much more. I really love people who go after their goals and dreams. Let's go after my goals and dreams more. I really love people who when we get together, we're able to talk about all different kinds of topics and we don't have to argue with each other. Let me be the person who's able to facilitate those kinds of conversations. I love when I'm around families where the children are able to speak their minds. They're treated like humans. Let me treat my children like humans. I love being around people who have a healthy relationship where the husband and wife love each other and respect each other. Let me do what I need to do to have those healthy relationships. Become someone you'd love to be around. Become someone who is a solution and not a problem. Become someone who people want to be around. You should want to be around you and not always trying to run away from yourself or always trying to escape your life. If you're trying to escape your life, then you're not being the person that you want to be around. You don't even like yourself, so become someone who likes you if you want people to like you as well. If you want to really find the people who are really there for you, then you better get really close with your real self. You better start acting like you're speaking your truth and being who you are, and don't allow anybody to cloud that.

F* the noise. People are always gonna judge you. You've got to remember that. People are always gonna have something to say. People had something to say when I was 13 and pregnant and when I got an abortion. People had something to say when I got kicked out of my mom's house every single time. People had something to say when I got pregnant again at 18 and I had my baby as a teenager. People had something to say when me and my ex-husband got into a big fight, lost our kids, lost our home, lost our cars and we couldn't even be around each other. People had something to say during every season when I was homeless and when I was broke, sleeping from couch to couch or sleeping on the floors. People always had something to say even when I was getting my life together and becoming a better person. People still had something to say, people still shitted and people still hated. People still talked their shit. F* it. Let them say what they gonna say because they never had to live your life one day in their life. Let them f*g talk! You know yourself best and you know where you're going best. F* that noise.

Let people judge you. It's better to let some people judge you as you really are in your authenticity than to try to change yourself to keep them from judging you and they still don't f*g judge you. It's better to be rejected. It's best to stand in your truth than to be rejected after you've changed your entire self just to try to get somebody's approval. That shit hurts when you've gone through super lengths to do everything and be everything that somebody says you need to do and be and then that version is not even true to yourself and when you show up, they still tell you you're not good enough. That sh*t sucks. But you know what doesn't suck? When you are yourself. When you stand with your truth and people say, "No, I don't want you around me" then I don't give a f*. I don't want you around me either. I don't give a fuck. Thank you. Thank you for saving me the time, the space and the energy of giving my time, my space and my energy to the wrong person; to somebody who's not aligned with me. When you stand in your authenticity, and people judge and reject you, it's okay because you know you're good at the end of the day because you know, this is me and if they don't like and accept me as me, that ain't my problem. It's theirs. Take off the mask, and take off the facade that you've been putting on. You don't need it. You've only been putting it on because you give too much of a fuck about what other people think. And I'm not saying we are ever gonna stop giving a fuck about what people think because, even though we try to give less and less of a fuck, it's still something that we give a fuck about. We're humans, and we're communal beings. But it's like, let's just do less and less of that. Let's take off the mask even more. Let's stop fooling ourselves. Let's stop playing with ourselves. Let's stop playing with our truth. It's better to walk around as my real self and not be liked as who I am by the wrong people who don't even need to be around me anyway than to walk around as a fake a*s version of myself, laughing around, playing around, jumping around and dancing around to a tune that I don't even fucking like, just to be approved by a MF* I don't even like. No, thank you. You're gonna get me and if you don't like me, that's okay. We ain't gotta chill. There's nothing forcing us to be around each other. There's nothing forcing us as there are billions of people on planet Earth. Surely if you don't like me, there's somebody out there who will. Surely if you don't want to date me or be with me, there's somebody out there who will date you regardless of if you believe that or not. I believe that for myself. So let me quit wasting and spending my time trying to change for you or trying to get you to change and see me. Let me respect myself and dive out and say no, thank you. I'm done.

Also get rid of the unhealthy competition and jealousy. Some of your best friends and some of the people who are the best for you, are people who you might be silently competing with because you try to be like them. You're comparing yourself to them. You're competing with them. You're jealous of them because they've made it to a stage in life that you have yet to reach. Don't be jealous of them. Instead, connect with them. Talk to them. Learn from them. To be jealous and to have unhealthy competitions with another person is to push yourself further away from getting what you want in the future. Instead, compete with your past self. Be jealous of your future self because she got it all and she's doing well. That person is out there and they're killing it. Ayye! But don't be jealous of the people around you. Instead, use those opportunities to get to know the people you see who have made it to a stage that you haven't reached yet. Well, what is it that you're really doing? Sometimes we feel bitter about the people around us who are succeeding, who are growing faster than us, and who seem to have things that we don't have. But instead of feeling bitter, you know, recognize that if she can do it, then that's proof that I can do it too. So instead of hating on her and instead of being jealous of her, let me go and connect with her and say ask, "I just want to know, how you are doing this. I remember when you were going through some of the craziest things in your life and it just looked like there was no way up for you. But now I see that you and your life have just changed so much and you are like obviously a better person now and you're killing it. You're doing amazing. Can you help me understand how I can be amazing too? Because your success is my success and my success is yours." You should ask these questions instead of being jealous, shitting and talking down on yourself or instead of being jealous shitting on and talking about another person. If we recognize and see that they can grow then we also can grow too. We also understand that another person in the position that we want to be in but we're not in yet is proof that we can get there and all we need to do is to connect with that person. So be careful of who you talk about. Be careful of who you mistreat. Be careful of who you're jealous of because that jealousy can poison your future. It can poison your ability to gain knowledge, insight, information, friendship and collaboration with somebody who may really have the juice and the sauce that you need in order to get to your next level.

I remember there was a time in my life in 2019 where I went to this event called Social Proof that was hosted by **David Shands**, and I met a girl named Destiny there. I was thinking at that time that Destiny was just like me; she was in the same position as me. We were young girls, and we kind of go after our dreams and stuff. So I started following Destiny online and I realized that Destiny had an opinion. I realized Destiny had a voice. I realized Destiny was killing it. But I was still a broke bitch. You know what I'm saying? Like I wasn't really broke, but I was just sitting there looking at myself and comparing myself to her. I was silently trying to compete with her whiles also jealous of her to the point where I didn't even want to hear her because I wondered how she got to this part where she had got all this influence. She had all these followers and she was able to live the life that she living. Like I literally was jealous of this girl for no reason because she was doing well and I thought she was somebody who was doing as bad as me and misery loves company. So when I realized that no she wasn't miserable, and I was jealous and started talking shit about her, I said to myself, "Why? Why don't you just go have a conversation with her? Why don't you go learn from her?" So I had to check myself and you know what I did? I went to one of her events and I paid hundreds of dollars, maybe even over $1,000 because I had my kids with me. We stayed in Atlanta for about five days. We went and did all kinds of stuff and I went to her event which was hundreds of dollars. I paid to go and sit down in a room with this person who I had been jealous of so that I could learn from her and so that I can ask her questions and can tell her that I really appreciate her for staying strong and staying true to herself because it shows women like me that we gotta compete. We don't have to be jealous. We can collaborate, and we can love each other. We can learn from each other, and we can grow with each other.

So don't stop your growth by being jealous of another person's growth. Like I mentioned before, if somebody else's grass seems greener on the other side, go sit with them to figure out what they're doing, and learn from them to get some of the tools and some of the strategies and the methods. Don't hate on them. Don't separate yourself from them. Don't gossip about them. But rather go sit with them. Talk to them. Pay for them to teach you something. And you might just be amazed at what you'll find. You might be amazed at how far you're able to go. You might just be amazed at the beauty that they can transfer into you, instead of thinking the worst of them; thinking negative, thinking that oh, they must have done this and done that to get to the position that they're in. When you stop that and you say, you know what, instead of judging and assuming that this person must have done some BS to get to where they are because I'm uncomfortable with my position and this person because when I see them, they make me face the fact that I'm really not doing what the fuck I need to do, go sit with them and learn from them. Don't burn your bridges before they are even built. Don't cut your options, and your opportunities from growing before you even have them. Take good care of yourself.

CLOSING WORDS

As you embark on this journey of becoming more of yourself and less of a people-pleaser, remember to ground yourself and become present in your body. Take a deep breath in, hold it, and let it out before you respond or make a decision that could negatively impact your life. Come back to your center where you can focus and think straight, and where you are not operating from a place of fear and scarcity, but rather from a place of empowerment and abundance, knowing that everything you need, you already have, and those who you are seeking are also seeking you. Speak life into yourself more often, affirming who you are and want to be. You are the first person to hear the things that you have to say, and the first person to believe them. Speak goodness into your life and those areas where you feel neglected or hurt. An affirmation that I had to use to get over the feeling that I wasn't worthy as a single mom was, "I am well beyond worthy, regardless of me having kids. Because I have kids doesn't take away the fact that I am a human, and a woman who deserves to be treated with love and respect, simply because I exist." I had to remind myself that my parental status is not some automatic qualifier for bad relationships or loss of love and respect in this life, regardless of if others agree with me or not. There will always be people who don't believe you deserve something because of a decision that you made in your past or your family income level, upbringing, etc. People who love you will show up for you regardless of your identifiers. The people who are right for you will respect you and be there for you. You don't have to argue with people or debate with people who refuse to respect our vision, boundaries, and point of view. We don't have to entertain those who make us feel less than enough. Remember that boundaries are the door to what we allow into our life. Set stronger boundaries when you realize that you aren't getting what you want. Find some space to check in with yourself and be sure that you protect what's important for you. These include your beliefs, values, ideas and opinions. They are all just as valid as anyone else. So long as your boundaries don't violate other people's consent or cause corruption and division, let people believe what they want and you also believe what you want. You don't have to like it, but you also don't have to entertain it.

In my case, the guy who I almost married in 2020, had different beliefs than me. I sat there and drained myself, and nearly drove myself crazy after every conversation I had with him feeling less than enough, tired, and beat up because I was trying to prove something to somebody who didn't want to hear it. I was trying to convince him that he should believe in what I believed when in fact, I didn't even believe it, which is why I was so caught up in trying to prove it to someone other than myself. We don't have to convince anyone to see what we see. We just need to see it for ourselves and the right people will come along.

Tools to move forward

To help you watch your thoughts and protect yourself as you unfold, I want to share this tool called "autosuggestion" with you. Autosuggestion is the process of making suggestions to yourself once you realize that a thought or action which doesn't belong to you is influencing you. By auto suggesting, you consciously choose to acknowledge your own ideas in place of the ideas you may have from others. As an example, let's think about moments where we find ourselves in positions where we are surrounded by people who seem to be in a higher position than us. It can be easy to bite your tongue and not speak up for yourself because of old narratives that say. "Who do you think you are? You only have [insert level of education, income, etc], and they have way more. What you have to say doesn't matter because they know more than you." It can be easy to fall into that cycle and loop of belief, however with autosuggestion you become aware of your thoughts and choose what to entertain. So instead of entertaining a fear-based thought, you might entertain a thought that says, "I'm blessed to be in the room with this person. It shows that what I have to say is worth being heard, regardless of my background or experience", and that relieves you of the discomfort of wanting to jump up and run away from the situation altogether or keeping your mouth shut when you really want to speak up. You become less of the kid in the classroom who feels like you're not smart enough to raise your hand and blurt out the answer that's burning inside of you and more of the person who owns that what you have to add or say is of importance, and even if everyone doesn't agree with it, that doesn't make it any less valuable or worth saying. You recognize that it's when you're able to show up for yourself that you are able to receive the most help, support and guidance as you grow. Autosuggestion is the way to directly give yourself a boost of confidence in a moment where thoughts that don't belong to you try to creep in and influence what you really want. Affirming yourself is training your brain to automatically begin shutting down thoughts and ideas that you do not own, as they come. This does not mean that you can't examine the negative thought and ask yourself why I am having this thought. I encourage you to challenge your thoughts and figure out where they originate from and whether it's a belief you truly hold or one that has come from someone outside of yourself which doesn't align with your goals. I highly encourage you to start changing narratives and depressive thoughts in real time. These thoughts tell you that nobody likes you, nobody loves you, and you're not good enough. Smash that shit and remind yourself that you are loved, liked, and beyond worthy for the right people in your life. The only people who don't like you or have a problem with you are those who likely are not right for you or don't belong around you. Reprogramming your mind will do you a lot of justice. It will allow you to say, "This person is just another human being. They are entitled to their opinions, values and beliefs just like me. Therefore, I can assert myself and my beliefs just as they do, without having to feel like I'm not worthy." You may not be worthy to them, but you are worthy to those who are on the same path as you and that is what's important when you are headed down the path that is most true to you.

Don't fake it till you make it.

A piece of advice that I wish I would've never taken is the advice to fake it till you make it. It's a bullshit way of life that pushes you further away from being yourself. You don't have to pretend to be someone that you're not, instead just go after the life that you want and start being the person that you really want to be in the future, today. If you've had enough and you just can't do this shit anymore, where you're showing up and pleasing everybody but your damn self, or basing your life and worth of what you can do for someone else, smash that, and go after the life that you want in real time.

Start speaking up for yourself today, start making decisions that are going to be of benefit to your future self today, and tomorrow and the next day, and keep making them until you get to a point where you can say, "This is good." That's a point where if you were going to die tomorrow, you'd be happy with the decisions you made in life. Start living a life today that will ensure that your future self isn't worried about your past self, but instead they are concerned with being their best for their future. Don't fake it till you make it. You don't need to put on a mask or pretend to be someone you not. You've been doing that long enough already. You don't need to do it because those who matter won't mind who you are as you are. It's mostly those who don't matter who mind. You are the one who gives significance and importance to other people. Choose who you give significance and importance to wisely. The journey won't always be easy. Sometimes you will need a village to carry you through, and other times you will need to be submerged in silence just to think things through for yourself and detoxify yourself from the opinions and voices of others. Either way, be true to yourself and believe that you deserve the lifestyle that you dream about and want, then do what it takes to make that a reality. Even if it means having tough conversations with those you love, distancing yourself when they cannot respect your boundaries, and even no longer interacting with those who refuse to treat you well.

Thank you for reading my book. I sincerely pray it helps you connect deeper with your true self.

Connect with me:

If you'd like to book me for an event, speaking engagement or as a coach, below are the ways that you can connect with me:

Instagram: @winningwithwini

Email: wini@elevatedcommunityco.com

Website: www.elevatedcommunityco.com

Thanks to a couple of our early supporters who wanted to be mentioned or leave a word for readers:

CONNIE MOSELEY - A word from one of Wini's first coaching clients under the Elevated Community brand: "Whatever battles you're facing right now, God knows, God sees and God cares. Be encouraged to keep going, keep overcoming, keep thriving by faith. God bless you."

ARVILLA BECKWORTH - Arvilla is the founder of AB Personal Development Firm and Single Mom Coach. She teaches single moms how to get ahead in life by creating better habits that unapologetically put themselves first, and she believes that this book by Wini Griffin is a great addition to anyone who needs to become a better version of themselves! You can connect with Arvilla via email at

arvilla@arvillabeckworth.com